Peter Krause

Margrit Kennedy

Architect for Ecology, Complementary Currencies and Social Justice

with lots of love
Declan Kennedy

Translated by Elisa Graf

CONTENTS

>>Take a paper napkin and make five holes in it, side
by side, so you can stick your fingers through it.
Looking at your five fingers from the top,
they don't appear connected with each other.
Yet glancing under the napkin, one sees
that the fingers all belong to the same hand.

And so it is with the people of the world.
Some believe they are on their own
and have no real connection with their neighbor.
While some know that we all belong to the same hand.
Whatever we do to one finger affects the entire hand.

There are so many things that seem to have nothing to
do with each other, though it's not true.
We should try to look beyond outer appearances.
Sometimes we have to lift the veil a bit.
Be curious. Not believe everything we are told. Below
the surface we can see what connects us all
even though we appear to be separate
and sometimes feel lonely.<<

Margrit Kennedy

Preface

One of Michelangelo's most beautiful, and at the same time enigmatic works, can be marvelled at in Milan. The master himself claimed that he didn't invent his figures but liberated them from superfluous stone, working tirelessly on them until the very end. One can imagine how Michelangelo continuously gazed at this block of marble, listening to its form in order to perceive what figure was hidden in the stone. He would work on it awhile, making visible what his senses had intuited.

This continued for ten years. Time and again in evolving stages, he observed, he listened, he sensed, he worked and he let go. But his Pietà Rondanini was never completed. Before that, death had taken the tools from his hands forever. Yet it is precisely in the fragmentary, in the non-finito of this sculpture that its beauty and influence lies hidden. The viewer is instinctively prompted to complete the un-finished work with his own imagination. Thus, what should be a perfectly designed stone figure remains an opportunity for a spiritual experience. A fragment yet reveals!

The life of Margrit Kennedy was an exceptionally diverse, eventful and effective one. In the eyes of the world she was an architect, ecologist and money expert – that's how she was known by the many people she "infected" with her enthusiasm for equitable money systems. From within, she was driven by a powerful urge to balance inequalities and develop better ways of living. She expressed this succinctly herself:

- It's clear that two strong forces have been driving me since early childhood: rebellion and the need for balance."

Two forces, the rebellious assertion of one's own will coupled with a keen sense for symmetry and harmony, mark the defining elements of every artistic endeavor. In sculpture, it is the powerful, purposefully guided blow with hammer and chisel, accompanied by a balanced awareness of harmony, as the form is revealed. Rebellion and the search for balance can also be seen in terms of man's work on himself and on the world. To carve the perfect form from an unrefined slab of stone could well symbolize the purpose of all human existence: observing, listening, sensing, working, and letting go. To write this biography, I spoke with many of Margrit's companions and was given access to various archived material, including letters that Margrit had written in 2008 for members of the family and her particularly close circle of friends. In them she shares her most important life experiences. I am very grateful to Declan and Antja Kennedy that I was permitted to quote from these texts for this book, because Margrit always speaks for herself.

About herself, she wrote, for example:

- It is important for me to bring things back into balance. To resolve imbalances. And not just theoretically. It is simply a kind of natural need of mine to strike a balance between feeling and intellect, between practice and theory, between female and male principles. It is clear to me today that the three main issues in my life are the imbalance between man and woman, between nature and man and between rich and poor. I would like to correct these imbalances. And I know that all three are closely intertwined and interwoven throughout the history of culture and humanity. When I encounter them, it awakens all my fighting spirit!"

Also, among the articles of her estate is the draft of a book she wanted to write. It was entirely atypical of Margrit to leave anything unfinished. It was always her goal to reveal the perfection and beauty that emerges in the process of a work. All the more remarkable then, that she surrendered to destiny, leaving a final idea, a final work unfinished. The title she had envisaged was "The Sellout of Democracy", and several chapters were drafted to illustrate the areas of life and the world where she perceived the greatest dangers to be. In this respect, this draft is an expression of her unbroken fighting spirit. At the same time, it arouses suspicion about what Margrit would have written in such a book. As Margrit's husband Declan once said, "it is conceivable that at some point it will be written by others". But it may well be that it will be left as it is. As a fragment.

An art critic once wrote about the Pietà Rondanini that it seemed to him "like Michelangelo's last great question to the stone that no longer wished to answer". Perhaps this also applies to Margrit's final draft for a book, which she wrote in 2013 – the last year of her life. And perhaps this reinforces the impression of what Margrit observed in the midst of her lifelong striving human beings with their infinite potential – good, just and balanced, full of strength amid life's joys and sorrows!

The Path of Life
(1939 - 1959)

It took a team of 28 horses to transport the precious rare find. Under the direction of the Electoral Saxon inspector David Frenzel, the men managed with great effort to transport a particularly beautiful, almost four meters long specimen of a petrified tree from Chemnitz to Dresden. This was in the mid-18th. century. Located in the foothills of the Erzgebirge mountains, Chemnitz had since developed into one of the most important industrial cities in Germany. Steam engines and locomotives were built here. The smoke, coming from countless chimneys in the foundries, made life difficult for its inhabitants. But this city had the highest tax revenue per capita and the highest net product of all the cities in Germany!

The petrified tree, which had been recovered from deep layers of rock, was a remnant from an ancient time. Throughout that earlier age (the Permian period), the area of the city of Chemnitz was still located on the equator and its climate was tropical. Volcanic activity in the region, caused by plate tectonics, repeatedly triggered earthquakes. One of these had sealed the fate of a conifer, whose fossil remains were now on their way to a natural history museum.

Up to the advent of the High Middle Ages, the Chemnitz area was still covered in dense forests. In 1136, Emperor Lothar III founded a Benedictine monastery there, which was granted market privileges a few years later. This marked the beginning of the city's history, which at the turn of the 20th century was designated a "factory and trading town" dominated by mechanical engineering and the textile industry. With over 300,000 people, life in the city was comfortable for a select few, as most of the inhabitants were factory workers.

Moreover, industrialisation and urbanisation created a number of specific problems, the greatest of which was a lack of housing. Thus, in 1928, inspired by the British cooperative socialist Ebenezer Howard, a decision was made to build subsidised housing in residential areas designed in the style of garden cities with courtyards. This was ingenious and innovative urban concept, including its approach to social conditions. Through cooperative structures and the granting of lifelong residential rights, tensions were diffused – and a new quality of life was established. From a historical point of view, this social project is just as remarkable as the *Kippermünzen*, a coin minted in Chemnitz at the beginning of the 17th century. These were interim coins with temporary validity, used alongside the usual thaler coins. They were thus a genuine complementary currency.

It was in this industrial and historically socially innovative milieu, founded upon what had formerly been volcanic ground, that Margrit Kennedy was born on November 21, 1939, the daughter of Kurt and Anne Hübner. Less than three months earlier, the German invasion of Poland had taken place, marking the start of World War II.

Childhood

Initially, the city seemed safe. As early as autumn 1942, The Royal Air Force had identified the "Kleine Ruhrgebiet" (the small Ruhr Valley) as a strategic target for aerial attacks on the civilian population, but the range of their aircraft was still too limited to accomplish this. When this changed in 1943, the Hübner family was evacuated to the neighbouring small town of Lugau. Kurt Hübner was a producer of conveyor belts, classified as important for the war. Consequently, he was not required to serve as a soldier on the front lines. This proved a blessing for the family, as Margrit's brother Reinhard was born in 1942.

At the end of the war, the family escaped the Russians by fleeing from Lugau to Kassel, where Margrit's mother's parents lived. Living conditions were modest, and the exodus itself proved at times a perilous adventure.

❖ As a child, I didn't perceive money as a significant issue in our family. We were starving during the war, and after it had as little around us as everyone else did. We gradually grew into the German economic miracle just like most everyone. My brother and I grew up during these difficult war and post-war years, but at least we had the privilege of a complete family. ...then there was the escape! For days we were on the road; for me as a six-year-old it was a terrifying adventure. My mother risked her life for a typewriter, during a raid in which Belgian soldiers took our last belongings. 'I won't give it up, they'll have to shoot me,' she had said, pressing the old Olympus firmly to her chest with both arms. I was so scared that I could hardly breathe. The patrol finally let us go – with the typewriter."

Kassel was already largely destroyed and the Hübners stayed at their grandparents' home, which had suffered little damage during the bombings. There they lived together with more than twenty other people. In this cramped setting, the four of them had to share just one room.

❖ The beginning was hard. It was a hard life; my mother had to be strict. Like so many mothers at that time, she managed unbelievable things with us children. In spite of the scarcity of that period, she always acted humanely, reflecting compassion. I remember, for example, how every Christmas day she would take us to the nearby barracks, where poor families were housed, and we would give the children clothing and sweets."

Margrit wore the same blue wool dress every day. It was washed every evening and ironed the next morning. And when it grew cold in winter, long sleeves were simply fitted under the puffy sleeves. This went on for many years, as Margrit's mother had bought the dress in far too large a size, sewing in a hem which then had to be gradually let out.

❖ The dress grew with me. I wore it for at least four years, from October to May. It seemed to last forever. I hated it!"

In order to adequately feed the many people in the household, the family tended a vegetable garden. Day after day, sweaty and on their knees, Margrit's mother and grandmother looked after the precious plants. Observing them, it occurred to Margrit that as a woman, she hoped to never end up like this, so restricted by kitchen duties and children.

❖ We lived in the same house until shortly before my paternal grandfather died: my mother's parents downstairs, we and our other grandfather upstairs. Grandpa Berlin – as we called him – worked as a janitor after he had been a captain and lost a leg during the Boxer Rebellion in China. Now he was living on his disability pension and told us the stories of his many travels. It was much later – it must have been 1957 as I was just starting high school, the twelfth grade – that my parents moved with us to another apartment."

The Formative Years

Now more than ever, in the period immediately following the war, it was vital for people to harness all their skill and strength to make a fresh start. Nothing was left and everything was needed! In 1946, Margrit's father and his father-in-law Georg Schellhas ("Grandpa Kassel") began repairing rubber boots and bicycle tires in their basement. After the war and their evacuation, this small workshop provided the Hübners with a new economic beginning. At the same time, it marked the founding of a company that would continue to flourish successfully in the coming decades, up to the present day.

The small basement workshop grew rapidly. Only one year after its start, it was relocated from the basement to a shed in the garden. Margrit's mother had meanwhile taken over the accounting tasks. In this "production plant", scarcely more than four by eight meters in size, increasing demand was met with diligence. The family's living room was quickly turned into the company's "office", where an accountant was also soon hired to handle the growing backlog of orders. On the 20th of June 1948, in the course of the nation's currency reform, a starting credit of 40.00 DM was issued to each and every German, which meant 160.00 DM for the four Hübners. Margrit would never forget this Sunday because her parents used all the money to first pay the accountant.

❖ My feeling as a nine-year-old was: something essential to our survival has taken over our home. But it was gone again in an instant, because the business took priority. It was to remain that way for decades to come. This is how the German economic miracle began for me; I witnessed it step by step through my family, as my father created his own firm. My father followed a few very basic guiding principles in building his business. Until the end of his life, he rarely worked with less than eighty percent ownership and was thus able to cushion all crises quite well. And he would always say, 'If I'm a little faster than the competition, a little cheaper and a little better, then I've got the job.'"

Soon, the shed at the end of the garden was also too small, and the workshop rooms had to be continuously expanded in the years that followed. No one had any idea then that the foundation stone was being laid for what would become a worldwide group of companies with many employees in several countries. The first steps were still straightforward, and the objectives realistic.

❖ At the end of the year, my father looked at the balance sheet to see if everything was going well and if there was anything left. Do we need to grow or are we on the safe side? He was hardly interested in anything else. He ran his business – one could almost say – 'intuitively'. My father was not interested in growth; he just wanted to feed his family and pay his people. But the increasing

> demand pushed him to expand. More and more customers came with new demands, and he had to respond."

During the early years, Margrit's father regularly came to the table for lunch. He then slept for half an hour before continuing to work until five in the afternoon. But his weekends were dedicated entirely to his family. Then the two children would go on extended walks, through the woods around Kassel with their father. They learned how to orient themselves in the countryside – how to find the right route, and how to distinguish poisonous from edible mushrooms. Their mother usually stayed at home and was happy for the few quiet hours she could have to herself.

And in the evening, when the collected chanterelles mushrooms and porcini were prepared, they shared the adventures from their excursion in the countryside.

It was a happy time for Margrit. The family's economic situation improved, enough so that they could afford a few more amenities. Eventually it was even possible for Margrit to have a second summer dress! At the same time, her parents were always eager to promote their children's talents. Margrit loved dancing, ballet and music, which she studied through private lessons. These were formative experiences that shaped her for the rest of her life. She had learned to get by with little and to remain content.

❖ This helped me enormously later, during my years of study and my first time in America, when the three of us had to live on Declan's scholarship alone. I've never experienced such periods of scarcity as a great limitation."

School holidays were something truly special, in that Margrit occasionally joined her father on his business trips. She then travelled to many big cities, like Munich, Hamburg and Cologne. On these journeys, they spent days on the road while still a young girl she had the opportunity to become acquainted with the big wide world.

❖ 'What is that?' I would ask when I saw an imposing building somewhere. My father would always answer with an air of confidence: 'The Ministry of Culture!' It always took me a few seconds to realize that he had made it up. Then we'd both burst into laughter, because I had once again fallen for his joke. Once I discovered a beautiful sweater in a shop window, which was also much less expensive than the sweaters in Kassel. I wanted to have it. But no! That was out of the question. Buying clothes was my mother's job. There was a very strict division of labour: she was responsible for household and children, my father for business. When we went out to eat, I could choose whatever I wanted. I could have eaten double portions of caviar and father wouldn't have batted an eye. But he didn't buy me the sweater. I still remember it today."

End of School and Start of Studies

Margrit's parents had dedicated themselves with diligence and perseverance to the establishment of the company. There wasn't much room in their lives for aesthetics or intellectual pursuits. And they lived according to the classic role model of the time, insofar as the man should be able to pursue his professional career with a certain independence, while the woman looked after *children, kitchen and religion*. Moreover, the interests of the company were always accorded the greatest importance.

At school, it was time for final exams. Margrit, who later remembered a high school as a happy time, chose as her main exam subject what she was particularly good at: mathematics and drawing. She wondered if it would be possible to combine these subjects in her vocational training. Her father had proposed a home economics apprenticeship for Margrit; this was intended to prepare her for her role as a housewife. While he chose his son to succeed him in the management of the company. But Margrit didn't agree with these plans – she wanted something entirely different, above all not to play the role of a woman in the traditional sense. This was one of Margrit's most important concerns in her life. The other was her wish to study architecture. Incidentally, the latter was something absolutely unheard of for women at that time – but Margrit knew this, and it made her all the more attracted to the idea.

Towards the end of the 1950s Kassel became home to the new spirit of the *Documenta*, held for the first time in 1955. It is important to note the impact that this initiative must have had at that time, as it restored artistic liberty after the stark oppression of the National Socialists. This "Documenta climate" was full of formative experiences for the young Margrit. Her encounters with artists were to play an important role throughout her life. So, it was going to be a degree in architecture. First, there were entrance examinations to pass. All in half a year, Margrit undertook the application procedures at various universities. She arrived too late for the entrance examination in Munich. Together with four young men who shared the same fate, she had only been given a place in the back row of the lecture hall. Her heart pounding, she solved the exam's problems and completed the application. They then waited four hours for the results, passing the time chatting with each other. And then, elation! Of the 400 students applying to study, only 70 were accepted, and Margrit, the young woman from Kassel, was among them!

❖ I took the four beautiful boys with mc to Café Luitpold, where my parents were waiting. I said, 'We all passed and want to celebrate. May I go out with my future fellow students?' Despite all my willfulness, it was still standard to ask one's parents for permission. At that time, I was only nineteen... My parents hesitated, but then they agreed – not without first thoroughly examining the young men. At four o'clock the next morning I came home. 'You see', my father said, 'Munich is too dangerous a place. It's out of the question.' This time there was no arguing. He just wouldn't let me study in Munich. He had his reasons. Above all, he wanted to separate me from my boyfriend, who was then studying in Vienna. His parents ran a jazz club, which my father didn't like at all. But I had passed the exams in Hanover, Aachen and Darmstadt. Of the three cities, the shortest route to Vienna was from Darmstadt, so my choice was made. In 1959 I enrolled at the THD: Technical University in Darmstadt as a student."

She was now a "student of architecture and building technology", but somehow still felt she was fighting a losing battle, as only 30 of the 4,500 students at the Technical University in Darmstadt were women. Even so, Margrit experienced her studies as a wonderful, satisfying time. She felt completely at home because she was able to devote all her energy to what she liked most: architecture offered her the opportunity to combine her artistic talents and interests with very practical tasks. She was soon elected as a representative in the AStA (students' union). It was important to her that among her many fellow students was the son of a neighbouring family who had already been studying in Darmstadt for several semesters and who had given her important tips for the entrance examination. But there was someone else she had noticed, because when she came back to Kassel in October for a visit after the first two weeks of her studies, she said:

- There are only two men who interest me. The neighbour's son and his Irish friend."

As a Woman

Margrit's sometimes rebellious yet balanced character was rooted in an inner vision of humanity and a good life. She didn't first have to acquire this through protracted development or experience; it was present in her from an early age.

Nevertheless, the facts of her outer life naturally inspired her to become more and more conscious of her own latent aspirations and goals. In this context, she recalled an early childhood experience that took place when she was about three years old, when she was forced to stand with her face to the wall in the corner "as punishment".

- ❖ I turn around, see my father standing behind me and look up at him sullenly. He lifts his index finger and says in a threatening tone: 'little friend, little friend!' And I answer defiantly: 'When I grow up, I'll also say 'little friend' to you'! For me, this little story embodies the first sign of my rebellious nature."

She also referred to this event as her earliest memory of her lifelong struggle with patriarchal structures. In truth it can be said of her struggle for equality that Margrit was truly a child of her time.

It's hard to imagine today what it was like during the post-war years, and even well into the 1970s, when gender inequality was still a very much a reality. In West Germany, during the years of its economic miracle, girls were significantly underrepresented in secondary schools, and it was no different at universities. Only one in three women was gainfully employed, though in accordance with the views of that time, there was a clear distinction between women's and men's occupations. In marriage, men were considered the head of the household, essentially depriving women of their autonomy. Until 1962, women weren't even allowed to open their own bank accounts without the consent of their husbands. Similarly, up to 1977, they couldn't take up any professional activities without their husbands' express permission. These facts characterized the general social milieu in which West Germans still lived. So, it's not surprising that a broad movement came into being, demanding urgent change.

Her Mother

At home, Margrit was very conscious of the outdated roles inherent in her parents' relationship, as well. Her mother's life was restricted to such a degree that Margrit felt compelled to develop an alternative plan for her own life.

❖ My mother was an intelligent woman. She had the best grades in school and would have received a scholarship to study chemistry in Göttingen if only her father had been able to pay for her board and lodging. That wasn't possible. He was a simple laborer at Henschel in Kassel. My mother never got over it. She would always tell us how she had to sell pianos instead of studying chemistry. She wasn't even allowed to go to the theatre alone, without my father's permission. My father was a German patriarch. Within her restricted radius, she sought subjects into which she could invest all her energy: she cultivated her inclination towards spiritual questions and medicine, she healed us with herbs, she knew which teas helped against which diseases. With her sweats and curd compresses and infusions, she dispelled every cold. I am still grateful to her today for the fact that we grew up without antibiotics and other medication that my girlfriends were treated with when they were ill."

The circumstances of her mother's confinement only changed many years later when she separated from Margrit's father. Finally, she was so free again that she was able to pursue her own path and make her own decisions. Thus she took up studies in psychology at the C.G.Jung Institute in Zurich, having been accepted despite the fact that she had no high school diploma. As the oldest student and a mother of adult children, she brought a wealth of life experience to her consultations e.g. for the mother of a child with a pronounced anxiety disorder, she devised a song that could be sung to the child, enabling it to heal within a few weeks. But as far as Margrit was concerned, this psychological gift of her mother's had its limits.

❖ I remember an experience on the tram as a child when I used to go shopping in the city with her. Mother radiated so much trust and love and compassion that strangers would instantly share their stories with her. Most of the time it was something very sad: the husband had died, the father had died, the mother was ill ... She would listen to everything and would suffer from it for days afterwards. I was terribly embarrassed each time. Even then I thought: it doesn't make any sense. It doesn't help people at all if now she's sad, too. I began to perceive the difference between pity and compassion. She was able to help nearly everyone but herself. That is still fascinating to me today. So many couples, parents, and women were grateful for her advice, support and healing. But she could not heal herself. For her it was true that it was only through suffering that one could grow. That was my mother's insight. And I didn't want to be that kind of woman."

Margrit once came across the idea in a work by Albert Camus that to be happy was much more difficult than to be unhappy. For it to be possible, one has to make an active effort. So, Margrit resolved to go down that more difficult path of happiness, in order to overcome her mother's conception of greatness through suffering. With this concern she was not alone among those of her generation, who were all seeking a different, more conscious relationship with their parents!

❖ It was precisely because I had rebelled so thoroughly and vehemently against the gender roles that my parents had presented to me, that I had to struggle with myself for a long time to really accept my mother as she was. But one day I woke up and suddenly knew: now is the time. Now I can accept her as she is. And for the first time, as never before and never again after, I experienced a moment of grace. With this, I realized months later, I also achieved the greatest psychic 'energy saving program' of my life. 'You sound so different, ' my mother said on my first call after the experience. She felt it immediately. 'Yes, that's right,' I confirmed, 'and that's how it should have always been.' But unfortunately, it hadn't been like that. Then she put me to the test. Her forgetfulness worsened. When we went out to eat, she would ask me at least seven times: 'What's the name of this restaurant here?' Then each time that I was able to answer, without the slightest reproach, without a trace of impatience, 'We're in the Crown Restaurant,' I knew I had really succeeded. So, we still had quite a nice time together. Three months. She died at the age of eighty-two."

School Years and Career Aspirations

While she was a student at a girls' high school in Kassel, Margrit had a teacher who she liked very much. This teacher, Dr. Ohnesorge, taught English, German, History and Social Studies. Margrit was deeply impressed by her, not least because she had survived in a Nazi concentration camp and was now working to ensure that such a thing would never happen again.

- ❖ But she also introduced us to Goethe. I owe her a great debt of gratitude. My ability to analyse; also the courage to stand on my own. She was a fascinating role model for me, and through her I still feel closely connected to Anthroposophy."

While still a young girl, Margrit began contemplating her future career. Her first priority was financial independence. She did not want to be dependent on either her parents or her husband in any way.

- ❖ I had experienced at home what economic dependence meant for women of the time. I always found it unfair what a free life my father led and how constrained, in contrast, my mother's life was. She would not have been able to get a divorce – at least in the first lean years, if she wanted for us to have a good education. That shouldn't be the reason to stay with a man, I thought. The thought of being at the mercy of a husband's whims without any earnings of my own was horrifying to me."

At school, Margrit stood out for her fine achievements in mathematics and art. Should it be these talents through which she could pursue a career? She herself excluded the option of teaching as a profession, because above all, she didn't want to become the "unmarried old maid" that her teachers appeared to be. She didn't want her future defined by her hardships in life, but by happiness and joy! What about a life as an artist? Margrit had always been a talented illustrator. But in the end, it seemed to her that her talent wasn't enough for a life as a professional artist. Besides, she already knew many artists in the Kassel *Documenta* scene at that time. And she didn't want to live their lives, as they appeared extreme and insecure. But then, in a short space of time, her destiny was revealed when it became very clear what goal she could and would dedicate herself to, with all her heart.

❖ In the second to last year – I was now eighteen – I had to make a perspective drawing from the Museum Fridericianum in Kassel for my final exam in art. My rulers were not long enough to reach the vanishing points outside the sheet of paper. My father had a brilliant idea: 'We're building right now. Ask our architect. I'm pretty sure he has such rulers.' 'No problem', said the architect. And he offered that I could work in his studio on the weekend. My desk at home, like my rulers, was much too small for the drawing. For the first time, I spent the weekend in an architectural office. The planners and draughts-men also worked on Saturdays and Sundays and were under pressure with their projects. I immersed myself in this atmosphere, had everything explained to me, and admired the concentrated, creative teamwork. And I knew: This is how I want to live! This mixture of art, aesthetics and reality had an almost magnetic influence on me. In our home, it was always about the company. When my parents invited guests, they were mostly my father's business friends. Discussions revolved around products, markets, sales figures and strategies. It was different in this architectural office. It was about form and function and their relationship to each other. It was about the balance between art and costs. It was precisely this balancing act that won over my heart for architecture. That weekend I discovered one of the fundamental needs of my life: creating balance. Balancing extremes. Finding the right, good middle point. By Sunday evening, I knew: this is it, I want to become an architect".

***

It was crystal clear to Margrit that she would reject the training in home economics her father had proposed. With only the best of intentions, he wished for her to assume the role of a housewife. But being wedged between home and hearth was exactly what she didn't want!

Even more difficult than solving the problem of her father's expectations was penetrating a profession that at the time was still typically reserved for men. It was only at the beginning of the 20th century that women were able to study architecture at all, and at the start of the 1960s still very few availed themselves of this opportunity. Many of them had previously completed vocational training or had come from the field of fine arts. And then, as architects, women mainly worked in the fields of interior design and residential construction. To make her dream of a career possible, Margrit had to assert herself in a largely male-dominated discipline and field of activity – and, above all, first prevail against her parents, who had envisaged something entirely different for their daughter.

❖ Back then, I had to use tears to get my way. But my mother was on my side. And in the end, father considered me a poor candidate anyway, because he was sure I would eventually marry. So, he finally gave in. From that point on, I answered the 'What do you want to be' question like a pistol shot: 'Architect!' Everyone would then say: 'I beg your pardon? That isn't possible. After all, it's a man's job.'"

As a Woman among Men

Whenever she was confronted with such stereotypes, it only increased Margrit's determination to hold fast to her career aspirations, despite all odds. She applied to study at seven technical universities. At four of them she took entrance examinations, qualifying as one of the top students. This bolstered her self-confidence, as it indicated she was on the right track. And it also proved to be a valuable experience for her future life.

- I understood that often things seemed complicated only in people's minds. This was a useful preparatory exercise for the money theme. Without this early training in the courage to say and do what I think is right, I would not have been able to take it up."

A few years later Margrit was thirty-seven years old, having already worked successfully as an architect for more than a decade, lived in Berlin and worked for the School Building Institute of the Federal States. She received a letter from Paola Coppola Pignatelli, professor of architecture at the University "La Sapienza" in Rome, describing her observation that male and female students designed very differently. She now wanted to know whether Margrit had made similar observations. Was it possible to differentiate between male and female architecture on the basis of their own characteristics?

At first, Margrit did not find this particularly evident, as there is no gender-specific physics or chemistry. But the enquiry had piqued her curiosity. So, she began leafing through a folder with old designs and eventually found what she was looking for. A drawing she had made in the sixth semester evoked memories from a characteristic situation. Together with two fellow students, she had set out at the time to produce sketches for a holiday settlement, to be submitted as part of a student competition between the universities in Darmstadt and Vienna.

Margrit now saw something in her design that could be construed as 'women's architecture'. She had designed a weekend house by a lake that had U-shaped rooms grouped around a staircase. It was an attachable concept that allowed one or more rooms to be used, depending on whether the rooms were for individuals or families. And now she was reminded of the collaboration with her two fellow students at the time, how they first developed ideas on their own, then discussed which idea was to be developed and submitted for the competition.

❖ I was sitting in my corner at the time and thought, Now, older people and people with children or without children will be coming to this holiday resort. So, there has to be a lot of flexibility. People who want peace and quiet must also be able to have peace and quiet. And those who might want to romp should also have the chance to do so. What they all have in common is that they want to enjoy the countryside and nature when they come on holiday from the city. We were finished by two or three in the morning. Heiner had not managed anything. When I saw Frank's design, I was shocked and speechless. He had designed an octagon, a terraced building in a bay at the northern end of the lake overlooking the water to the south. It was a multi-storied building that reached with one story into the lake; it housed public facilities, such as shops, doctors' surgeries and a dining room. It was an unusual, modern, futuristic solution at the time. 'Who wants to live in that?' I asked, 'People come from the city! They may as well stay at home: people above, people below, people next door... Where is the free space, the recreation, the connection to nature?' He looked at my drawings: 'Well, I'd rather have my holiday in your design, as well', he said, 'but we'll never win the competition with that'. It was a point that only interested me as a second or third consideration, but as I later discovered again and again, always came first for my colleagues. We decided to let our professor choose the next day which model to pursue. Prof. Schwanzer from Vienna only glanced at the two designs, pointed to Frank's and said: 'This one!' I felt a sting. That was yet another one of those many small defeats I suffered during my studies. And which shaped my image of myself as an architect. I hardly had any female colleagues to talk with. I was surrounded by men – as fellow students, as professors. And, of course, Frank was right. His motivation was clear: he wanted to win the competition. And I was 'only' interested in thinking about how people could live well in a building and how they could be connected with nature. These approaches are simply worlds apart. And as our professor had opted for Frank's design, I thought my design was simply not good enough. It confirmed my fear that I wouldn't be a good architect."

A curious feature of this incident is that another working group had taken up Margrit's design and submitted it for the competition. And they actually took first place! And now, many years later, the experience of that time spoke to her in a new way. She realized that she hadn't fought sufficiently for her idea and that she had given in too hastily. She conveyed the oppression she'd felt, as she "kept herself small through these countless experiences in her everyday life as a student". It made her absolutely furious!

❖ Because suddenly, at the age of thirty-seven, I came to see how I had allowed myself to be constantly undermined by these men. For so long, I thought my questions: how does one move in the space? What does one see when one looks out? How can social interaction take place here? ...were irrelevant! No one understood at all; everyone around me, 98% of them men, had a completely different concern. Their priority was: what does it look like from the outside? It should be as large and impressive a form as possible. Monumental! To prove that architects are great artists. Up to today, this is still for me the key difference between male and female principles – and not only in architecture. No sooner had I discovered and formulated this and sent it to my Italian colleague, my mother called. I told her what I was doing, at that moment. 'That's interesting,' she said, 'haven't you read the book 'Childhood and Society' by Erik Erikson, that American psychologist? There's an experiment where children, shortly before puberty, were asked to build an exciting scene for a film using building blocks, through which Erikson wanted to identify the problems children have during puberty.' 'Yes and?' I ask, slightly irritated. 'What does this have to do with female or male architecture?' 'Ninety-five percent of girls built caves in these experiments, and over ninety percent of boys built towers.' I read the book and thought: It's really strange that, fully independently, having not thought of it even once all these years before, I now perceive my design from the sixth semester as female architecture, and this story of the competition with the holiday resort, as well, and that it corresponds perfectly to what girls design. Isn't that crazy?"

"Everything's possible. You just have to want it."

From this point on, Margrit occupied herself more and more intensively with the subject of "female architecture". And as she delved more deeply into it, the more background and experience she was to gain. Telling her friend, documentary filmmaker Helga Redemeister, about her research one day, she in turn shared an observation she'd made at an apple juice factory in Bavaria, where she witnessed children playing with empty juice boxes: the boys were building towers and the girls were building caves. The filmmaker had taken several photographs of this activity and now left them with Margrit. This marked the beginning of Margrit's collection of materials and literature. She also studied the works of Cäcilia "Cillie"

Rentmeister, an art historian involved with matriarchal building forms.

Gradually, Margrit came to be an expert in female architecture. In this capacity, she conceived a double issue on this theme for the German architects' magazine *Bauwelt*, which also contained a longer article she wrote herself. Contrary to all expectations, copies of the issue completely sold out shortly after its publication.

In 1978, two architecture and urban planning exhibitions took place in Germany, both organized by women, illustrating the concept of female architecture. One entitled "Women form their city" was held in Bonn, Zurich and Darmstadt. While the other, in Paris, featured designs by women from 22 countries, under the title "Women architects exhibit." These events proved to be as successful as a 1977 exhibition "Women in American Architecture: A Historic and Contemporary Perspective", which captured the attention of many in major American cities.

In the focus issue of *Bauwelt*, Margrit explained that she was not concerned with the assertion that "one is 'good' and the other 'bad'", but that one-sided dominance of the male principle is our key problem, as evidenced by the impoverishment and destruction of our natural environment. In seeking to espouse and implement holistic principles, men as well as women face the same barriers produced by the millennia-old devaluation of female principles.

As an expression of female principles, Margrit described in her *Bauwelt* contribution an architecture that "develops as a result of individual and collective needs in harmony with local building materials and traditions in a growth process in which 'male' (formal) principles are formed in close connection with topographical and climatic conditions". This already hinted at what would later occupy her intensively in the sense of ecological building, because consideration for ecological aspects were for her a very specific expression of female architecture.

❖ This was another one of those milestones along my path. It gave me courage once again to say: 'Everything is possible. You just have to want it'. The success of my actions has helped me to endure the fear that of course was also there. I remember very well that when I published the Women *Bauwelt* magazine in August 1979, I thought: 'Now you'll never get another job.' I had a hard time conquering the 5000 years of patriarchy in me, but the time was obviously ripe for it, because the opposite happened. There was a huge response and fierce debates, and I was invited to give numerous lectures. Just a few months later I was offered a job at the IBA. It was already a small victory against all predictions that I had studied architecture at all. The fact that I was able to take up this theme, discuss it in public and still continue to work on it further strengthened my courage. And my confidence grew so that I could formulate what I didn't like about the world, and find people whom I could convince, initiating change. Unfortunately, I didn't produce a book about it. At the time, I was more interested in how it could be implemented: how could I promote women at the International Building Exhibition, the IBA-Berlin of 1984, where I now worked. Right from the start, when providing information about the subjects I was employed to work on ecology and energy, I would add, '...and women's projects', because at the IBA, I once again encountered pure patriarchy."

Her father – the business man

Her parents

Parents

Margrit, with her mother and brother,1942

1946

With bother Reinhard and grandfather
from Berlin Oscar Hübner, 1953

1954

Carefree and Open for Everything New (1960 – 1978)

Evidently, the first impression was indeed the best, that first moment Margrit met the great love of her life. It was while visiting her neighbour's son in Darmstadt, an important and trusted ally among the unfamiliar surroundings of the university, that she first met Declan. Both were immediately taken with each other. Then they danced together at the faculty Christmas party. And when Declan visited his friend in Kassel afterwards, a walk with Margrit led to a memorable conversation.

❖ I remember it as if it were yesterday. Suddenly there was a pause: 'Margrit, I have to tell you something: I'm just a big flirt. I don't want to get married.' And I shot back, 'Thank God! Finally, someone who doesn't want to get married. I'm so relieved, 'cause I feel the same way'".

That was the beginning of a lifelong bond – and a successful, happy marriage!

Darmstadt and Regensburg

Many professors teaching at the Technical University, Darmstadt were well-known in their time. These include Rolf Romero, who had specialised in the reconstruction of historically important buildings in the post-war period, and Ernst Neufert, who was still working with Walter Gropius in Dessau and whose book on the measurements of the elements of building design had defined new benchmarks in the field of building standards. Neufert also, however, had a National Socialist past which, similarly in the case of Theo Pabst, did not initially attract much public attention. It was only after Margrit had already completed her studies that Pabst got so caught up in the mill of the critical student body that he – a man who had twice been dean of the Faculty of Architecture – had to resign from his teaching post, worn down by the hostilities he had suffered.

Among Margrit's professors was Eugen Kogon, whose seminar "The Future of Unbelief" she attended in 1960. The course dealt with a topic of intense interest to Margrit and Declan. By this time Margrit, the daughter of a Protestant family, and Declan with his Irish-Catholic background were already on the path to a church-independent, free worldview. At one point called by the university's president, Johann-Dietrich Wörner: "the moral conscience of the university", Kogon had stood up against National Socialism as a sociologist and political scientist, and as a result had been imprisoned for several years in the Buchenwald concentration camp. His book *Der SS-Staat: Das System der deutschen Konzentrationslager* (The SS State: The System of German Concentration Camps) had, since its publication in 1946, become a standard work on the crimes of the National Socialists, and was distributed worldwide in various languages. Margrit and Declan were impressed by his thoughts, particularly his ideas for new, free and social forms of society.

However, the wild times of the 1968 movement were still relatively far off, and Margrit's studies proceeded along classical conventional lines. Gradually, she acquired the knowledge and skills needed to be an architect. Among the highlights were excursions that gave the students practical insights into architecture and its history. In 1960, for example, the students took a trip to Vienna lasting several days. Margrit and Declan thoroughly enjoyed these days in the time-honoured city. They were in love, going to the theatre and out dancing once the "official" sessions of the day had finished. The nights were short, but with the *joie de vivre* of those newly in love they endured the lack of sleep.

In winter of the same year, on the 17th of December, they celebrated their engagement. They had bought the rings in Paris. Declan came to Margrit's student room that day, before the annual Christmas party of the Chair of Architectural History and Design, where they made their promise to each other with a small ritual and two glasses of champagne. Shortly afterwards

Margrit became pregnant, so the wedding was celebrated in Kassel a few months later, on the 4th of April 1961. Out of consideration for Declan's family, the wedding took place in the Catholic rite, and a Spanish priest friend had been invited. He had arrived from Vienna on the night train, completely exhausted. The wedding party was forced to wait quite a while in the church, the "Mary Queen of Peace" – a modern church building, which the couple had chosen especially for the day of the wedding – until the priest had finally had enough sleep. It was a beautiful celebration – as beautiful as the coming decades of their marriage were to be.

Yet a small shadow was cast over the young couple's happiness; Margrit was disappointed that she couldn't take advantage of a Fulbright Scholarship she'd been granted to study in the USA. In those days, the Fulbright Scholarship was a particularly important symbol for the fostering of international cooperation, because in the post-war world, it was essential to promote the reconciliation of nations in all aspects of life.

For this purpose, specifically to encourage academic exchange between the world and the USA, the Democratic politician James William Fulbright developed and launched a scholarship program that is still one of the most prestigious in the world today. Fulbright himself had been able to study in Great Britain before the Second World War as a Rhodes Scholar and had not forgotten this great experience.

Now he was able to use part of the proceeds, from the sale of surplus war material not returned to the USA, to promote academic education and the peaceful exchange of knowledge across all borders. Margrit had applied for such a scholarship – and was granted one. But now she was newly married and pregnant. Declan comforted her and promised that a study period in the USA would still be possible at a later date...

And then in October 1961 their daughter was born. Declan was in the final stage of his studies, and so the birth took place exactly at the time of his exams.

❖ Antja was a perfectly healthy, easy child. Wherever we put her, she slept; when we picked her up again, she laughed. It all worked out wonderfully. We always shared the family duties very well, actually. But, naturally, it was also a constant learning process in terms of gender roles."

Before Antja's birth and a few months later, Margrit and Declan had made trips to Greece, where they saw clearly that they were deeply connected to this country and its culture. Throughout their lives, this experience would resonate and their connection to Greek culture continue to evolve. All in all, travel played an important and recurring role in the lives of the Kennedys. Margrit even spoke of a "great migration" that began for the family in 1965.

The "great migration"

It wasn't always easy for Margrit to reconcile the demands of her studies with her married and family life. Sometimes her parents came to Darmstadt to help in the household, or they took the child into their care in Kassel. This even made it possible for Margrit, during her studies, to design a school center which was built in Nigeria. Declan's brother, who worked there as a missionary, had arranged this. Although Margrit did the work for free, the flight costs were covered, as well as board and lodging. But the most important thing was the experience Margrit gained there as a young student and the fact that she was able to show a first, valuable reference project. In addition, through this project she had found a topic that would continue to occupy her as an architect for many years to come.

In 1965, four years after Declan had passed his diploma examinations, the Kennedys moved from Darmstadt to Regensburg. Declan had been hired for the restoration of the historic city center there and was only able to spend weekends with his wife and child in Darmstadt, throughout the first year. That had now come to an end. After Margrit also received her diploma in 1966, she began working in her profession, at times as a freelancer and at others as an employee.

In Regensburg the Kennedys were doing well. They were comfortable. Through Declan's work under the guidance of the ingenious Prof. Dr. h.c. Werner Hebebrand, Margrit gained an impression of urban design and regional planning, which was so engaging for her that she decided to continue her education in this area. At that time the Kennedys were renting a house in a good neighbourhood, right next to the Schuster family, whose new house Margrit had designed. It was a wonderful, vividly intense time. The special friendship between the families still exists to this day!

After a short time in Regensburg, there followed a move to Dundee in Scotland, which had become a major city during the 19th century due to the growing jute industry. In the early 1960s, the city underwent extensive redevelopment, as a result of which many historic buildings disappeared. Declan found work as a senior lecturer at the "Duncan of Jordanstone College of Art", teaching urban design.

❖ We had bought a house right on the waterfront, in Broughty Ferry, overlooking the Firth of Tay with St. Andrews behind it. It was a dream. It was our first house together, and considering our circumstances at the time, we invested a lot. We thought it would be worth it for five or six years, and maybe we would stay longer. But it only went well for two years. At first everything was sunshine. The Head of School had hired four young assistants: a Dane married to a Norwegian, an Australian living with a Latvian, a Scotsman living with a Swede, and then this Irishman with his German wife. An exciting, international team, and the eight of us were quite good friends among ourselves. But all

> the people in the architecture department said: 'This can't go well', because this head of school was an egomaniac. Over time he became increasingly jealous of his assistants, who were much better received by the students than he was. He could not stand that. Within a short time, the team was completely split, and all four assistants quickly looked for other jobs."

The years in Dundee weren't easy for Antja either. While her father could finally live and teach in his mother tongue again, the English language was still quite foreign to her. Declan recalls how, at first, she used to speak to her dolls in a gibberish consisting of both German and English. At the strict old-fashioned school, the language problem caused the little girl considerable hardship. Once she was hit on the hand with a ruler because she didn't answer a teacher. But she had not understood the question at all. And all the other children in the class kept silent...

USA

Just at the time the working conditions in Dundee became too difficult for Declan to bear, he was offered the chance to study for a doctorate in "Public and International Affairs" in Pittsburgh. This not only meant liberation from the strained social conditions of his job, but also the opportunity to keep the promise he had made to Margrit to live and study in the USA at some point – now quite soon. Oddly enough, through the Urban Affairs Program – a joint project of the Graduate School of Public and International Affairs and the Graduate School of Public Health – Declan became a doctoral student and professor at the same time. He taught urban design in the Mid-Career Women's Program, where Margrit later completed her master's degree.

As convenient as the timing was, the move was difficult, because at first Margrit and Antja had to live on their own in Scotland, after Declan had already gone to the USA.

❖ I not only worked full time – even then I was designing schools, a primary school and a technical college – but also looked after our daughter, while managing the sale of the house and the move. While packing, I had to handle every letter, every book, every piece of clothing. Since we had to pay for the whole move ourselves, every kilo of weight counted."

And then there was the task of getting the sale of the house off the ground, which proved not so easy. Margrit had tidied everything up and made it beautiful to make the property appealing to potential buyers.

❖ I can only assume it was a Scottish Sunday amusement at the time, to inspect properties for sale. I led countless tours and was always extremely friendly. And people were always delighted with our sanctuary. 'Such a warm house', they'd say. And that was true; we had night storage heaters, when most houses there were still heated by open fires. Each time I thought, 'They'll buy it now.' But no. It went on like this for months, and there was a point – after I had also survived the party for Antja's eighth birthday – when I was so exhausted that I couldn't even get up the stairs. I literally crawled up into my bedroom."

Eventually, when the sale of the house had at last succeeded, it was possible to get underway. First, they drove with their old Citroen to Kassel, where they exchanged it for a new VW. In the fully loaded car, they drove back to Southampton to embark for New York. After a five-day crossing on the S.S. France, the largest passenger ship at the time, they finally arrived on the 23rd of December 1969.

❖ Declan picked us up at the port. Our furniture had been transported in a wooden container on the same ship. We had to pay the people on the quay the same price that it had cost for the entire crossing of the container from Southampton, just to lift the container from the ship onto the truck using a forklift. Declan had never driven a truck in his life and now he had to drive this monster, first through Manhattan. I drove with Antja in our VW, which we'd also brought on the ship behind him to Pittsburgh, Pennsylvania. Not exactly the dream of a big city. At first, this city, especially the slums around downtown, was truly horrible for me."

In Pittsburgh, Margrit was nevertheless soon better. She recovered quickly from the strains of the preceding weeks and again relaxed. The furnishings in her new home were quickly improvised, as Margrit wanted everything to be reasonably comfortable for Christmas, which was fast approaching. Beds were created out of the wooden crates that had been used to pack their furniture and bricks, and various furnishings were obtained from the university's household furnishings collection.

Only six weeks after her arrival, Margrit found a job at the UDA office (Urban Design Associates). The owner of the office, David Lewis, was a young, successful South African who worked as a district planner but also in the construction of turnkey houses and schools. Margrit's prior knowledge of school construction came in very handy. The collaboration developed well – and Lewis became a friend of the Kennedys.

The office later took on too large a project, then encountering payment difficulties. This was a thorny situation for the office's 18 employees and on top of that, no salaries were paid for three months. Yet such a situation reveals the value of a good working atmosphere: the whole team continued to work undaunted – and thus saved the company from bankruptcy.

Soon after Declan completed his doctoral studies with an ABD (All-But-Dissertation), he was offered a part-time position as associate professor at the Graduate

School of Public and International Affairs. And when Margrit got a scholarship for the Mid-Career Women's Program, she was finally able to start her studies in Urban and Regional Planning. She was very thirsty for education, studying simultaneously in different faculties (among others, gaming as a planning and teaching tool, programming, psychology, urban affairs). She and Declan had previously agreed that she would subsequently follow up with her doctoral studies and the actual dissertation, because due to the financial burden this was only possible for one of them.

On the whole, the Kennedys' recipe for marital success was, rather than each for himself, to strive together to live in the most balanced and conscious way possible. Each was to be allowed to pursue their own interests, and neither was to impose limitations on the other through their own particular lifestyle. They made sure that at times Declan's, and at other times Margrit's interests were at the forefront. To achieve this end, they had many discussions, and at times even argued with each other. Yet purposefully and with great effort things worked out. The idea to create a marriage contract, to be renewed every ten years, came from the renowned US ethnologist Margaret Mead, whom Declan had met in 1963 in the context of his work in Ekistics. Margrit and Declan adopted this idea, first implementing it in 1971 during a trip to San Francisco. After this, they applied the concept time and time again.

The private life of the Kennedys was characterized by the fact that Margrit and Declan were always seeking friends, everywhere they went. They liked community and were always receptive to new, fresh ideas and perspectives. Antja remembers many such discussions having reflected this spirit of culture and tolerance.

***

After three years in Pittsburgh, it was once again time for a change. Despite good contact with a wonderful circle of friends, Margrit and Declan still didn't really feel at home. The atmosphere of the city was not as vital and progressive as they had imagined. What's more, Margrit was keen to participate in the political life of the community more than was possible for her, as a German in the USA. They began to consider the prospect of working in Germany, and soon found a job posting in the trade magazine "Bauwelt": the Technical University of Berlin was advertising for a "Professorship for Infrastructure in Urban Development". Declan applied – and seven months later had the contract in his pocket. His first attempt ended successfully in a full academic appointment!

After that things went pretty fast. Declan moved to Berlin with Antja – who was thrilled to get the last spot at Berlin's bilingual John F. Kennedy School (JFKS) – while Margrit continued her doctoral studies in the USA. At the same time, she continued her work in David Lewis' urban design office, renowned for its extensively participatory design processes.

- This was the beginning of a phase in which I worked a lot on the participation of stakeholders during construction projects. I also wrote my master's thesis on the subject of 'Education and urban planning as congruent events'. There were special scholarships at the University of Pittsburgh, to help women re-enter professional life. I had remained working, but I got this mid-career scholarship anyway. The scholarship winners were an incredible group of women. Black, white, young, old. A colourful mix. It was the first time I really appreciated working with women. Most of them already had a lot of work experience and wanted to get back into the business or get ahead. I really enjoyed that. It was an incredible opportunity to learn, outside of architecture, everything that is important in the context of the social sciences. We were never taught this in our studies in Germany. During this time, 1971 to 1974 at the Graduate School of Public and International Affairs (GSPIA), I was able to develop my broad, networked view of things, which was later so useful for the theme of money."

Margrit was able to read and learn very quickly. She worked methodically, reading texts quickly and understanding them immediately. This proved to be of great benefit to her, as she was able to complete her (second) degree in a short time. After completing her master's thesis in 1972 and passing the oral examination, she went on to do her doctorate, which she completed in the short space of just three semesters.

***

In the meantime, Declan had found a small flat along Fasanenstraße in Berlin, from where he could walk to the Technical University. Later, when Margrit had arrived in Berlin from Pittsburgh, they were able to move into an apartment that had just been vacated. There was clearly always a fair amount of luck at play!

Antja spent the first few weeks at the private Kantschule, as the John F. Kennedy School was closed during American summer vacation. Finally, the time arrived that she could switch schools. But it was a long way from the center of Berlin to Zehlendorf. In addition, Antja was considered an American at JFKS, which created certain identity problems for her. Should she feel like an American because she had recently received a US green card? Or an Irish girl, because she had a passport from there? Or as a German because she had been born in this country? It was again a "mess" as she had experienced so often before, through all the many moves.

Declan was very involved at TU Berlin, and this meant that he sometimes forgot very mundane things around the household. In the evenings he might even forget that it was time for his daughter to go to bed. All this gave Antja a lot of freedom, which made her ever more independent.

In those days it took a long time for letters from Germany to reach the USA, and telephoning was still very expensive. Nevertheless, mother and daughter talked to each other on the phone usually once a week. But the longing grew. As hard as Margrit tried her best, she missed her child and husband. As a result, she became downright ill. Finally, Declan came to visit her, and taking care of her as best he could, nursed her back to health. Antja had also come with her friend Tobi, so mother and daughter were together again for a while. But this beautiful time soon came to an end.

❖ When we brought the children to the airport, I had to go straight back to the hospital on the way home. Afterwards we took a few days off and I tried to tell myself: 'It's getting better, yes, it will definitely get better'. But it didn't get better. It just got worse."

So Margrit decided she would write her doctoral thesis from Germany and move to Berlin.

❖ I had delayed following Declan and Antja to Berlin for one year. I received a doctoral scholarship immediately after successfully completing my Master thesis. For this I also had to, at least part of the time, remain in America, because before one could submit a doctoral thesis there, it was necessary to pass twelve exams. These were in, for example, systems analysis, urban anthropology, social psychology, organizational theory, administrative theory, sociology, urban and regional planning, legal foundation – everything to do with public and international affairs. In other words, quite a lot. But ultimately I was also able to write my dissertation in Berlin."

Berlin

The year of Margrit's move to Berlin, and one year after the publication of the book "On the Limits of Growth" by the Club of Rome, Ernst Friedrich Schumacher completed his book "Small is beautiful". Soon after it was published, Margrit and Declan received this book as a gift from Declan's father. In it, Schumacher calls for a radical rethinking, to achieve maximum happiness with a minimum of consumption. Accordingly, he urges a restructuring of the economy bringing it back to a human scale. At the time, Margrit and Declan were already engaged with ecological issues and the consequences arising from them, but the clarity and systematics of Schumacher's thinking impressed them very much. The ideas they came into contact with at this time were a powerful stimulus and inspired their work over the rest of their lives.

Although the family was now reunited and living in comfortable circumstances, they had to get used to each other again, after living a year apart. Antja had become an independent young lady who had quickly learned to follow her own path. This posed a particular challenge for Margrit.

- Then came the most difficult time ever with Antja. In that year of separation, she had grown accustomed to handling everything with Declan on her own. While I was in America, he had taken her as often as possible to all the social events. So, in the first few months when there were three of us again, I had to wage a few battles with her to override certain 'privileges'."

Declan took a more relaxed view of the way Margrit and Antja adjusted to living with each other again. He had benefited from having grown up in a large family with many siblings, while Margrit's views on the parenting of their daughter were shaped more by the conservative austerity of her parents' home. Due to his "Prussian upbringing", her father lived by clearly defined ideas about roles, which also defined his relationship to Margrit. That's how it was at the time. There was much for Margrit's generation to overcome and transform. Thus, it was fortunate that Margrit had become a mother so young, as being closer to her daughter in age meant that they were able to do a lot together, when Antja had become a teenager.

***

In addition to the very private, loving side of Margrit and Declan's partnership, their exchange of ideas in their professional fields, and their work on projects together was equally impressive. In 1974, they collaborated as editors in the tastefully designed book "The Inner City," the 14th yearbook in a themed series on urban design. The previous three volumes "The

Pedestrian in the City", "Urban Structure" and "The Growth of Cities" had been edited by David Lewis.

The year 1974 brought yet another move, though still in Berlin. The Kennedys had found an apartment on Nassauische Straße in Wilmersdorf, in the same building where the sculptor Waldemar Otto, was living at the time, and whose daughter was a friend of Antja's. One of the most important modern protagonists of figurative sculpture, Otto had studied at the Hochschule für bildende Künste (Art College) in Berlin. Already highly regarded as a sculptor, he was appointed a professor at the Hochschule für Künste (Art College) in Bremen in 1973. Waldemar Otto gained international recognition through various awards, residency programs and exhibitions, for example, in Ireland, Chile and in the Hermitage in St. Petersburg.

The Kennedys now had plenty of room in the large, former garrison apartment. Declan was even able to install a grand piano again, as the apartment was big enough for that. Nevertheless, Margrit found it difficult to really feel at home in Berlin.

❖ Declan had meanwhile been elected as the second vice president of TU Berlin and worked a fourteen-hour day. Our friends were all his friends, and they were only marginally interested in my topics, i.e. school construction or participatory processes, then later the topic of women and architecture, and even later and sometimes in parallel the topic of money. They talked about what Building Minister XY and Mr

So-and-so were doing, but I didn't know them. So, I couldn't join in at all. Yes, at times I also suffered from not belonging anywhere, because of this jet-set lifestyle. But, of course, it gave me a broad worldview that I wouldn't have acquired in any other way."

There were often, at every possible opportunity, discussions on serious and ecological matters. Declan and Margrit were at it constantly. As some of it was also very disturbing, Margrit was unable to let things go and had trouble sleeping. This was also because she wanted to get to the bottom of every issue. Yet as much as Margrit's interests were linked with the community, she had little interest in becoming politically active. She had tried that once before but proved too impatient when it came to meetings; she was always interested in action rather than words. Later, when she had become a professor in Hanover, she was approached to work with the Greens and immediately refused. Long-winded laments were simply not her thing, and crucial discussions should, in her opinion, always be held with those directly concerned. This is how she was remembered by those present, when later, at a meeting of Steyerberg's local government on the subject of the district's heating supply, she left the room visibly angry at the fact that the public was not sufficiently involved.

***

After selling their house in Pittsburgh, Margrit and Declan purchased a small semi-detached house in Berlin. They had searched long, touring a variety of houses for sale – as after all they were both architects, and therefore had very specific ideas about their prospective new home. They then found what they'd been looking for in the district of Schlachtensee, not far from the John F. Kennedy School. The house was accessed via a quiet residential street, the Waldsängerweg, lined with old houses that had survived the war, as well as new buildings in various styles. The surrounding residential area is abundant with greenery and the Schlachtensee lake, a popular excursion destination for Berliners, is not far away.

Margrit and Declan renovated the house to their specifications before moving in and lived here between 1977 and 1985. A large window was installed overlooking the small garden at the back of the house, providing an unobstructed view of an uncultivated green area covered with a variety of pioneer trees, which directly adjoined their own small garden. A grass roof, still a novel and unusual feature in those days, was also installed.

From the house it's a short walk to the shore of the lake: Schlachtensee. Margrit used to jog there daily to recover from her work. In the first year she wrote her doctoral thesis from home. The living room became her workplace. And as there were no computers back then, in addition to a typewriter, there were also the many, many pages and notes of her written work. For her research, Margrit worked a lot with games that she played with children in different countries. This was, as she said, the language in which she could best communicate with the little ones. The multitude of notes she'd made on this also lay on her desk in her living room workspace. For Margrit, who loved order, this at times posed a real challenge, but it was no problem for Declan and Antja.

In the course of her doctorate, Margrit made numerous trips to different countries around the world. It was a rewarding, and exciting time for her; she always came back revitalized and inspired. She gathered and developed new ideas which flowed directly into her work, devising the concept of schools as community centers. These shouldn't be places for only dry school lessons, but places where other cultural uses are included – even beyond the exclusive use of a building as a school.

***

The topic of schools as community centres occupied Margrit for many years. It was reflected not only in her master's thesis but also in the dissertation that followed. As a result of her expertise, she was engaged from 1974 to 1979 as a research associate and consultant at the School Construction Institute of the Federal States in Berlin as well as for the school construction departments of UNESCO and OECD.

❖ The School Construction Institute had sent me to Paris in 1974 for a UNESCO conference on schools as community centres. After that I received a research assignment from UNESCO. When I presented the research results to UNESCO at a school construction seminar at the OECD, the OECD's school construction department also wanted me to work for them, which was unusual, as the two departments were geared more towards competition than cooperation. So I ended up working for three institutions on the same topic, and it wasn't always easy for me to meet all their demands."

Ultimately, Margrit was now not only involved with the projects of the School Construction Institute of the Federal States, but also with those of the OECD and UNESCO in Europe, and North and South America.

❖ Through my research reports, I soon had an infinite amount of material. This was one of the hot topics of the 1960s, and there was a time when probably no one in the world had more material on the subject than me. My first senior project in college was a design for a technical high school in Obagku near Owerri, Nigeria, in 1964. I went there with Declan at the beginning of the Biafra war and drove through the crisis area with my brother-in-law. Then I designed two schools in an office in Scotland. At Urban Design Associates in Pittsburgh, I went on to design schools as community centers in various large and small American cities, Pontiac, and Ann Arbor Michigan, Cincinnati, Ohio... The central question has always been: How can this school facility, which exists in every village, in every city, and which is normally used no more than fifteen to twenty percent of the time, be combined with other uses to achieve better utilization? The variations were endless – and yet there were similarities all over the world. I was commissioned by the OECD and UNESCO to collect data in fifteen countries in Europe and North and South America. During these years I collected information from more than fifty countries around the world. And this work with UNESCO and the OECD has of course given me a very broad horizon of knowledge about what is really going on at the local level – from Scandinavia to South Africa, from Canada to Japan and Indonesia. It was an exciting time. And then I found it even more exciting to extract and formulate the most important things from these very differentiated and complex experiences. At first, I thought that the traveling was the most exciting part, but when you analyze it and write it down, it quickly gets rather boring. I soon realized that it's the other way round. In this jumble of material, what is now here that could be useful to others?"

***

Every so often, Declan and Margrit would interrupt their daily routines by putting on a record and dancing with wild abandon. As well as the new rock'n'roll music, joyful freestyle dancing to a good beat amplified the exuberance. Antja remembers dancing as an essential part of the family culture. But the spouses could also argue well. Margrit was at times a rather harsh critic. Despite all their passionate fury, they always sought to find a common denominator on which they could reconcile.

Just how easygoing and open to everything new Margrit and Declan could be is highlighted in an anecdote from this period. Antja had registered for a workshop at the Tanzfabrik (Dance Factory), but due to illness she was unable to attend it. Margrit and Declan decided to go instead, returning home wildly enthusiastic. As a result of this excursion, they'd gained their own access to the Tanzfabrik, which played an important role in Antja's life. Later even the grandparents from Kassel attended the public performances there!

The Tanzfabrik also featured in Antja's moving out of her parents' home. As it was such a long way from Schlachtensee, and because Antja often didn't come home until late in the evening, Margrit agreed that her daughter should move in closer into the Tanzfabrik's large shared flat.

Their daughter's departure was one of the important events of 1978. Another was the purchase of a house on the Greek island of Hydra. Margrit and Declan had actually planned to do this together with Marlene and Lars Gustafsson, who they had met when Lars, a respected Swedish writer, poet and philosopher, had lived in Berlin for two years as a DAAD scholarship recipient. However, Margrit's father had warned so strongly against jointly purchasing a house that the Kennedys eventually bought it on their own. The house was idyllically situated 440 steps above the harbour, facing north. It was beautiful, though not ideal for Margrit, because the sunsets she so loved to watch could not be seen from the house. Nevertheless, the Kennedys spent many very full and wonderful holiday periods there, alone or together with friends. The connection they felt with the island and its people was so strong that Margrit and Declan even considered making it their main place of residence, to pursue a small farm as a project for permaculture and participate in the ecological development of the island. With their ecological expertise, they became involved in community affairs wherever they could, for instance, in forest maintenance after a large-scale fire that could not be efficiently put out, because traditional cisterns had previously been destroyed.

Social Architecture and Urban Planning

With her Dipl.Ing. (MSc,) in Architecture Margrit was already an experienced architect at the age of 33. She returned to school to get a Masters Degree in Urban and Regional Planning (M.U.R.P.) at the Graduate School of Public and International Affairs at the University of Pittsburgh. In her thesis, she investigated the particular conditions related to the construction of schools, with which she had become so familiar in previous years. Her firm conviction was that schools should not only be places where knowledge is imparted, but also centers of cultural and community life.

Master's Thesis

On the basis of three dimensions, she divided her work into three parts: Part I deals with the overlap between education and urban planning, Part II deals with institutions, agencies and specific trends in these areas, and Part III deals with the environment or social context in which dimensions I and II exist.

Before writing her master's thesis, Margrit had been engaged with efforts to integrate black and white children in two schools, in Pittsburgh and Pontiac, Michigan. Through this work, she became aware that schools can only be pedagogically effective up to a certain size. The school in Pontiac had 2,300 students. So how, she wondered, do urban planners come up with an idea of what school is needed in a particular place? This question arose from practical experience, because as a consultant to the Board of Education in Ann Arbor, Michigan, she had witnessed time and again on new school construction projects that there was a lack of coordination between planners and education authorities. Consequently, the plans were often obsolete before they could be printed. And, therefore, she questioned, how it would be possible to remedy this clearly flawed process.

Initially, holistic plans were referred to as "visions", illustrating how future challenges could be met. In the 1960's, there was really no general theory of persistent social change. This only emerged with corresponding developments in the 1970's. In this context, Margrit developed her own approach – novel and innovative at the time – which methodically addressed the people concerned, in order to involve them as participants in the planning process. Throughout her life, she remained committed to this basic concern of involving those affected in planning and change processes, in all aspects of her work.

Her master's thesis was initially aimed to illustrate which social dynamics move a society from one form to another, identifying the effects these changes have on institutions, as well as the concerns they raise. And she noted that in the widely held view of the future, we are either alarmed by the development of total control determined by our interpretation of the past – or we dream of total freedom. It is therefore necessary, according to a key statement of her master's thesis, to understand that freedom for every individual cannot be maximized without a certain amount of planning and control, requiring a balance between individual and public interests.

To achieve this, bureaucratic and institutional structures must be overhauled and changed. If we expect institutions to maximise people's freedom, we need to define the parameters for planning and governance, balancing individual interests and public authority. Perhaps even more important is the preliminary determination that the institutions must change to serve in the interests of freedom and the intended system of democracy. Thereby, the pervasive experience of the democratic process (sharing, voting, delegating) can be used as an instrument in the restructuring of hierarchical institutions.

The tendency for educational and planning institutions to compete with each other demonstrates clearly, and in detail, a move from rigid control to maximum flexibility, and from hierarchical to horizontal management structures. Margrit's analysis illustrates –

through a simple graphic of two overlapping circles, with the most important area of overlap shaded – how the interests of education and urban planning overlap as corresponding events. This simple graphic draws attention to a process of particular concern to Margrit, leading to a question of vital importance to her: how can citizens be involved in decision-making processes, so that their needs can truly be identified and considered? In practical terms, Margrit suggested that simulations, planning games and preliminary tests be carried out for this purpose.

Using Ann Arbor, a town with 100,000 inhabitants, as an example, she outlined in more detail the concrete problems that can be resolved. Like many cities, Ann Arbor suffered from a common process of deterioration of which both its citizens and institutions were well aware. In such a situation, Margrit believed that schools have a central role to play in the search for solutions, as places of encounter and exchange for the interests of local citizens. This raises awareness of the relationship between education and urban planning. It is important to know all the related facts. Otherwise, she says, one should not even start the planning process.

What is problematic about the traditional methods of planning, however, is that many aspects of communal living are approached in a too technical manner, whereas flexibility and quick responses are more important, for which a good social database is necessary. It is possible to create such a pool of valuable information if a model of decision making based on participation is applied. Simulation is very well suited for this purpose, where citizens face information and problems that affect their daily lives. It has to be made easy for people to participate in such a game. The rules of the game must be easy for everyone to understand. The success of the game is determined by whether or not it's fun to play. And most importantly, mistakes must be allowed.

As reasonable as this idea of enabling participation in the game is, it's difficult to achieve, as there is a tendency in formal education and research to detach issues from the concerns of society. However, education needs this practical reference in order to preserve the feeling of solidarity. In her closing remarks, Margrit summarized this in a statement that remains valid to this day:

❖ The public school system which in the past has failed to prepare people to recognize and deal with the problems they are facing today, now has a unique chance of initiating a new philosophy in combining its efforts with those of other urban planning institutions to a more powerful trust against ignorance, alienation, frustration, and non-involvement in setting up a decision making process, in which education and urban planning become congruent events."

Doctoral Thesis

Margrit began writing her doctoral thesis in1973, under the title "Community schools: The Potential and Limitations of a Concept", submitting it to the University of Pittsburgh, Graduate School of Public and International Affairs in 1978. This thesis was basically a follow-up to her master's thesis, the content of which she had further developed for her doctorate, supplemented by numerous other research results and conclusions. As the connection between the educational and social sectors has become increasingly important to society on the whole in recent decades, her dissertation dealt with the very topical subject of state administration.

During the period up to the First World War, the secularized state had replaced the churches as the most important educational institutions in Germany and comprehensive reforms of the education system had been undertaken time and again. This reflected efforts worldwide to achieve a minimum level of education. The traditional "community schools" of the USA could increasingly be found in Africa, Asia, Europe and Latin America. Margrit had set out to examine and compare the concepts and experiences in the various countries.

In doing so, she benefited from all the experience she had gained while working as an architect planning community schools in Nigeria, Scotland and the USA. She now focused on how community schools were established, how concepts were developed and implemented, and what role the planning process played in all this. In particular, she argued, the planning process could be a way to overcome the traditional isolation of schools in the community. The experiences gained in many places, both positive and negative, could eventually be drawn upon for future projects.

During her research, it soon became apparent that using technical means to pursue social goals didn't always produce the best results. A different approach was necessary, for example, in meeting the task of integrating different ethnicities and classes, coordinating administrative activities and reviving community life. In her dissertation, Margrit showed that this can only succeed in the context of extended development strategies, because this is the only way to capture the significant influence that emerges out of the most diverse relationships between a wide variety of actors.

Some of the school projects carried out in the 1960s did not correspond to actual needs and requirements, because the administration was based on centralization rather than through an actual network of local relationships. In contrast, in some countries in the 1970s, there was a growing trend towards smaller, decentralized projects, which was supported by progressive developments that had already transpired in society as a whole during the 1960s. The aim was to appropriately respond to an increase in the number of pupils and the associated need for new schools, which could potentially be used not only for teaching children and young people, but also for adult education and other community purposes. In this way, Margrit concludes, primary and even secondary schools would indeed become "community schools".

In order for this particular opportunity to be recognized, the coordination of planning processes between various institutions is necessary, as well as the development of methods to support a wide variety of partners in the joint development of plans. While revisiting the complex themes she had addressed in her Master's thesis, in her dissertation Margrit continued to work on what she considered her most pressing concern: the need to make transparent democratic processes the basis for all planning and design of the social sector.

It's just as interesting to see how carefully Margrit included in her planning the resources in the vicinity of the schools: the people, nature and cultural facilities. Today this holistic approach would be seen as 'sustainable', while at that time the term was not yet so widespread. The fact that planning processes have since become increasingly more transparent – which was as yet a real novelty at the time – is likely due to the spread of environmental thinking. Margrit deduced from this the need for a study that would indicate which methods are particularly suitable for making networked planning possible.

The Theme of Building Settlements

In 1993, Margrit participated with Doris Haas and Friedrich Gnad, in writing an investigative report entitled *Zukunftsweisender ökologischer Siedlungsbau in Europa* (Future-oriented ecological settlement construction in Europe), which was then published in the reference book "Successful approaches to urban and village renewal in terms of traffic calming." The authors were concerned with the question: How do larger ecologically oriented housing projects (not initiated by the residents themselves) actually function? The need for such an investigation arose as more ways were sought to transfer the experience gained in smaller projects to large construction projects.

The study was based on seven completed projects in six European countries comprising more than 1,000 residential units. From the 1960's onwards, healthy building gained increasing recognition, and in the 1970's the first houses were constructed using healthy building principles. In addition to the choice of location and recyclable building materials, the focus was now also on environmentally compatible living in terms of energy generation and use. But, this necessitated an awareness that was not much in evidence among the general population in those early days of the ecology movement. The reservations with which these new ideas were met were correspondingly widespread among the public.

Educational and PR work was needed to make the new ideas accessible to everyone. In the study, Margrit found that in the context of housing development, the potential for the application of ecological solutions is greater than in the construction of individual houses. This made ecological building attractive for municipalities and cities.

The results were presented to the public in Barcelona, in the spring of 1994, at a workshop organised by the European Academy for the Urban Environment. It's easy to imagine that the participants were very impressed by the presentation – especially as, at that time, interest in ecological forms of housing was steadily growing among the population. Margrit therefore specifically emphasized that "the image boost for cities, builders and architects through the realization of ecological settlements is invaluable."

Undoubtedly, the study reflected the wisdom and many experiences Margrit had gained in her years of re-building Lebensgarten, the eco-village in Steyerberg – particularly in relation to early involvement of future residents in planning processes.

To Margrit, ecological building and living simply make sense because they are social processes. She wrote:

- Ecologically oriented settlements – and this is one of the most important statements of our research – can also be planned on a larger scale, financed as social housing and successfully implemented.

Particularly with regard to larger settlements, some ecological goals can be implemented better or more effectively than in smaller ones (e.g. freedom from traffic, noise and danger, etc.)."

As a continuation of the progress report on future-oriented sustainable settlement construction, which was primarily about ecological settlements, a report followed in 1996 on "Renewal" (Volume II) and "Urban District Projects" (Volume III). Again, the topic was examined with a view to projects in various European countries (Denmark, Germany, the Netherlands, Austria and Switzerland).

Among the co-authors this time was Declan Kennedy, who had conducted various interviews with officials and residents as well as site visits together with the Danish architect Tony Andersen, and who had also been intensively involved in renovation and neighborhood projects for many years.

For the purposes of comparability, the selection of projects for Volume II focused on countries for which new construction projects had already been previously examined. One of the main differences between the new construction and renovation projects was that the study found that, in contrast to the ecological settlement projects, less clear guidelines had been developed in connection with the renovation projects.

Nevertheless, it could be shown that:

- ecological measures are possible when converting larger building complexes
- traditional architectural and urban planning principles can be positively assessed from an ecological perspective
- ecological conversions are not necessarily more expensive than conventional ones
- and that the public sector plays an important role in supporting such projects

Likewise, the special commitment of those living in the renovation projects was emphasized, who realized a "social art" during the realization, which shows how much Margrit was always also concerned with the awareness of the cultural processes that are to be understood as part of the ecological meaningfulness of a project.

She also pursued this objective in her presentation in Volume III, which presents three selected projects, the "Solar Village" settlement in Pefki Lykovrisi in Greece, the "Garten City Puchenau II" in Austria and the "New Building in the 7th District" in Vienna.

Female Architecture

Another of Margrit's very important concerns was what she called "feminine architecture". She had come to realize that the feminine in architecture is an essential quality of its own, one that had previously received little or no attention. As well, she recognized the building forms of the modern era as an expression of male dominance – and thus of a social constitution that absolutely must be overcome.

In 1976 Margrit attended a lecture in Berlin by Carlo Aymonino, who was then Dean of the School of Architecture in Venice, Italy. During this lecture, she had a memorable experience in relation to her work on female architecture.

❖ For two hours he showed his designs: grandiose forms of concrete in the play of light and shadow. No tree, no man, no animal, nothing living appeared in his pictures. I had just visited one of his projects in Milan. A residential complex, with incredibly long lines of buildings, where downward winds whirled shreds of paper and plastic bags through the air, and the people coming around a corner were under sudden threat to be blown away. For me, this was not architecture for people, but rather architecture that was sufficient in itself as form, without taking the human function into account. At the end of his lecture I asked Mr. Aymonino whether he had ever asked the users of his projects what they thought of them. That's a strange question,' he replied, 'someone asked me that the other day in Aachen.' No, he didn't, and he didn't care. I couldn't help myself – I probed again. Then finally he angrily replied, in front of the hundred or so experts in the hall: 'Well, you sound just like my wife. She always asks me questions like that!'. That night I lay awake for a long time. It was one of the typical sleepless nights I would often experience later. They are truly the most creative ones – especially when something moves me deeply! This one was highly creative. I wrote an angry letter to Mr. Aymonino, saying that he was of the opinion that women and their concerns belonged in the kitchen, and that architecture that fulfilled a function was not art, etc. It was yet another struggle with patriarchy, my furious rebellion against injustice between the sexes. I sent the letter first thing in the morning, as an open letter to him and to the *Bauwelt*, one of the leading architectural magazines in Germany. Conrad Ulrichs, the editor-in-chief at the time, published it in the next issue and afterward received more letters to the editor than ever before. The overwhelming majority was of the opinion: 'A really great letter! At last women are finally having their say!' This was also written by many male architects who didn't subscribe to this kind of architectural doctrine."

Through the *Bauwelt,* Margrit received a letter to the editor that particularly pleased her. In it, the French architect and founder of the international organisation of women architects, the "Union Internationale des Femmes Architectes" Solange Pauline Eugénie d'Herbez de la Tour invited her to the opening of an exhibition of women architects in Paris.

As women were not accepted into the International Union of Architects UIA, they had founded their own organisation and were now hosting an exhibition for the second time. Since Margrit happened to be in Paris at the same time for an OECD meeting on school construction, she was able to accept the invitation to the opening. She was eager to see if women would actually design differently than men – but was deeply disappointed in the end.

❖ The whole exhibition was nothing more than proof that women can design just as 'well' as men. The message was: 'We are just as good as you', especially among Russian women architects, who had apparently already had the opportunity to realize large-scale designs and who already made up more than half of the professional architects working in Russia."

Yet there was one exception among the female architects represented in the exhibition. The designs by Claude Häusermann-Costy appealed to Margrit. She wrote down her name with the intention of seeking a dialogue with her. She also resolved to write something on the subject of "Female Architecture".

❖ Just before I wrote my article, we took a vacation to Hydra in Greece. A friend, who was visiting us, invited us out to dinner. We went to the restaurant, and he kindly welcomed a woman and introduced us: Claude Häusermann-Costy, the architect from the Paris exhibition, the only one I really wanted to meet. 'I've been trying to contact you for months', I said, greeted her joyfully. 'I want to write an article on male and female architecture and would like to show some of your designs in it.' She immediately waved: 'Oh please, do it without me. I'm not interested in that.' I was a little sad, but I could understand her. After all, it had taken months for me to acknowledge that if I followed my own priorities, I would actually create something completely different."

With Declan in Ireland, 1960

Wedding in Kassel, 1961

With daughter Antja, 1964

With Declan and Antja, 1964

1969

1972

1973

Technical Professions Boarding School,
Ogbaku, East Nigeria, 1966

Architectural model, Hotel at Pillersee, Austria, 1965

General Training Centre and Industrial Rehabilitation Unit, Dundee, Scotland, 1969

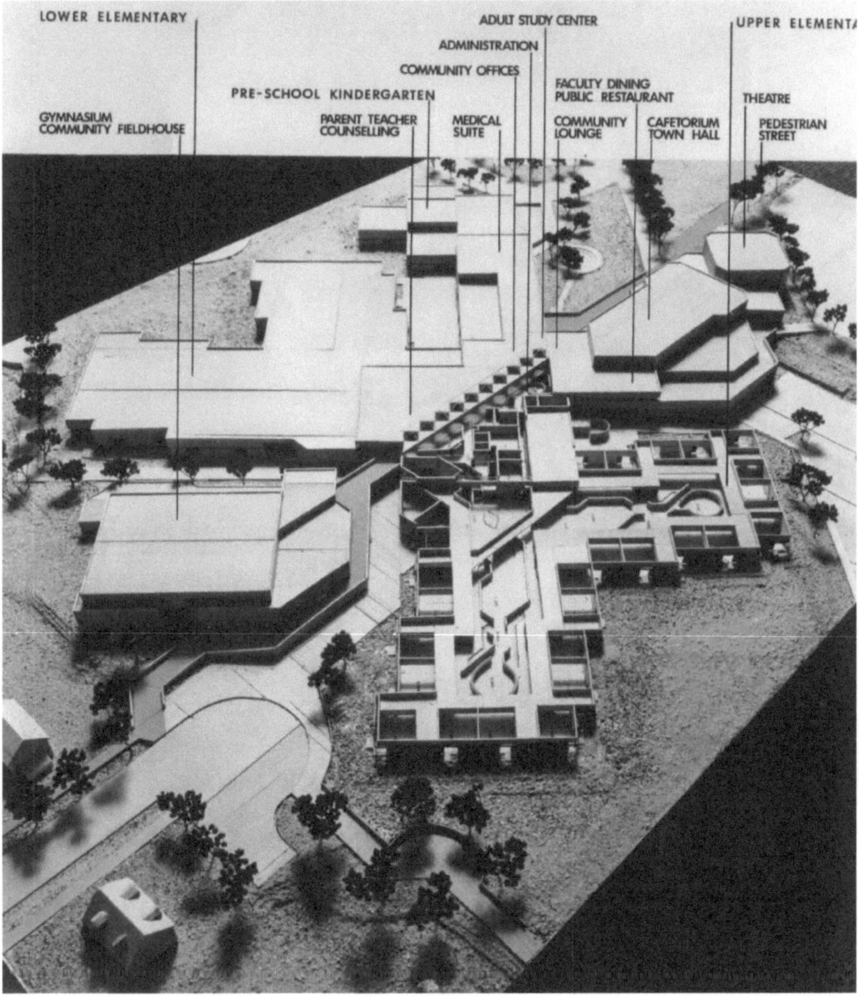

Human Resources Center, Pontiac, Michigan, 1970

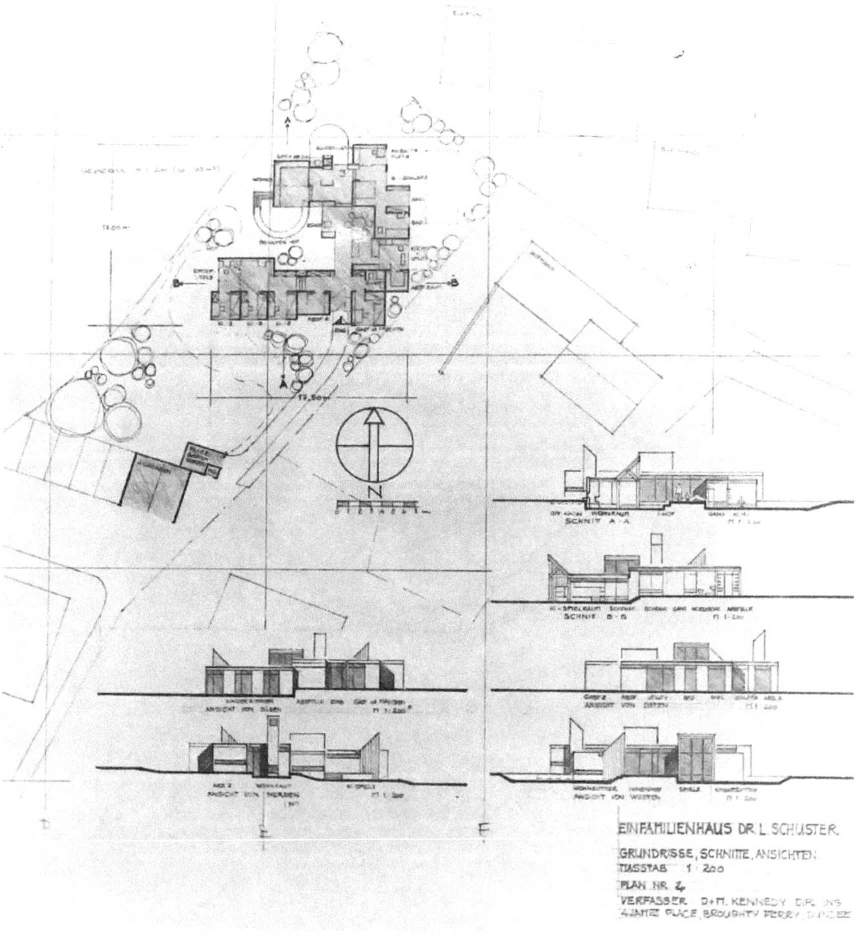

Schuster House – Design, 1969

Schuster House,

Margrit's Sketch of daughter Antja, 1962

And of animals in the Zoo 1963

Animals on the Farm, 1964

Ecology and Economy
(1979 – 2001)

Throughout her life, art and culture always played an important role for Margrit. She was herself a very artistic person. She drew well and in her own inimitable way. The drawings of animals she sketched illustrate her characteristic strokes which capture the essence of their shape. These are true works of art! And she attached great importance to a tastefully designed environment, both in her professional life and privately. She shared this fine sense of good art in common with Declan, and whoever meets the Kennedys can't help but be impressed by the balanced, artistic beauty of their home environment.

It was essential to Margrit's very nature that throughout all the years of her life she continued to meet people who were competent and respected in the artistic fields. As a young girl, she experienced the art scene connected with the Documenta in Kassel, but even later, important artists were always very close to her. For example, the American object and concept artist Edward Kienholz, whom Margrit came to know in the late 1970s through Lars Gustafson. An interesting and inspiring exchange of ideas soon developed with Kienholz and his wife Nancy.

In the meantime, Margrit was busy with her doctoral thesis. She had just taken a year off from her work for UNESCO and the OECD. This gave her the peace and quiet she needed to write her dissertation. It was a complex task to process all the research results that she had collected over the years from many countries around the world. During her many trips, Declan and Antja had stayed at home most of the time. Only now and then, during school holidays had they been able to accompany Margrit. Now this stage in Margrit's life had come to a conclusion. The subject had been explored thoroughly – and exhaustively.

❖ By the time I had written my doctoral thesis on the subject, I was completely fed up. When all the formalities connected with the dissertation were finally completed in America, I could no longer bear to hear the term 'school as a community center."

International Building Exhibition in Berlin

Six months later Margrit successfully applied for a job at the International Building Exhibition, Berlin (IBA). Due to her ecological orientation and her doctoral degree, she was immediately offered a five-year contract. Right from the start, she was able to add the topic of women's projects to the Ecology and Energy research area assigned to her, thus creating space for one of her most fundamental concerns. During the years leading up to 1984, this expansion of her responsibilities led to some particularly characteristic and meaningful outcomes, especially as she had long been interested in what she defined as "female architecture". She was deeply committed to support this, against all odds, in her new working environment.

❖ There were the most incredible stories. Women's requests were ignored, postponed, ridiculed. Everywhere I began to interfere, went to meetings, put pressure on. I had to listen to comments – from the head of the new building department, in the decision-making bodies – such as: 'Oh, you know, Mrs. Kennedy, I don't need women's projects. I already have a wife.' I wasn't very quick-witted back then. It wasn't until the evening, in bed, that I came up with the right answer: 'Why do you still build houses at all? You've already got one.' But I achieved my aim a little later. This man was so controversial, as head of the new building department, that the Berlin building commission felt compelled to organise a hearing with the experts in Berlin. About two hundred experts took part. For one of these meetings I organised the experts I knew: I called together all the women who were involved in IBA projects and said: 'Now is the time to open your mouths. Otherwise we can forget it. This is our chance to make public the values and goals that are important to us!' I made arrangements with the moderator so that the women could all present together, after lunch. Through the press, I had called for a 'women's sit-in' for half-past one. The event was to continue at two o'clock. When the men came back from lunch, all the seats in the hall were occupied by women. And the men had to stand in rows of four, along the walls – around this huge room full of women."

Outside, in front of the Building Commission's headquarters, the police had taken up position, anticipating an uncontrollable riot. But things went very differently! Inside, the female architects rose from their chairs, one after the other, to speak in their own words about family-friendly floor plans, child-friendly urban planning, the participation of women in the planning processes, urban greening, air improvement and noise protection. This sparked a wave of enthusiasm, not only among women, but very soon among many men as well.

❖ The hearing process was divided into two sessions, with the women presenting in the second session. The first session was about ecology. There was an ecological expert who was prepared to report on how the head of the new building department was internally undermining the ecological concerns of the IBA. She had forbidden employees to take part in seminars on ecological building at all, yet she stated in all published material that she took this issue extremely seriously. However, the expert who wanted to clarify this failed to say anything critical of this obstructionist policy, instead concentrating largely on his own ecological approach – when I realised that nobody could see what was really going on, I stood up in the hall as an IBA employee and said: "You are lying to Mr. K. when you say that you support ecology. You forbid your employees to come to ecology symposia. You have not held a single ecological competition, nor have you awarded any contracts or hired an ecologically oriented architect. Let me make that clear.' The experts in the hall clapped for minutes, but it was already evening. The allotted time was up, and the moderator ended the discussion. Afterwards – I will never forget – the then Building Councilor of Wilmersdorf came up to me and said: 'If it were up to me to award the Nobel Prize for moral courage, you would get it." Today I know that with this man, whom I fought so bitterly, I was waging the battle against my father. When I realized this, I forgave him and myself and apologized to him."

***

After her high school graduation in 1979, Antja took a trip to Brazil to visit her uncle Reinhard, who had established a branch of the Hübner company there. When Margrit finally arrived to supervise as an architect a construction project for the company, Antja translated her mother's words into Portuguese during the project meetings. In this way mother and daughter were able to work together productively, supporting and helping one another.

Despite her professional commitment, Margrit was always very attentive when it came to her family's needs. Antja was making the transition to her professional life, having initially decided to study environmental technology. Margrit had been able to find her an internship through her IBA contacts. But later, Antja decided to study dance. Margrit was completely open-minded in her attitude, and assured Antja of her full support, regardless of her choice of study.

***

In 1980, "North-South. A Program for Survival" – a report created by North-South Commission was published. Headed by Willy Brandt, the commission comprised a group of experts from various fields of science and politics, who had worked together in the three preceding years. The report aroused public interest - but it attracted the particular attention of those who were already concerned with a "green" approach to the world. And Margrit had been one of these for years already. From today's perspective, it can be said that the Kennedys and their work have made a significant contribution to the growth of the environmental movement, both in German speaking countries and internationally.

Two years after the publication of the report, on the occasion of Germany's admission to the UN, Willy Brandt gave a speech to the UN General Assembly. On the subject of what he later called "world domestic policy", he said: "People are becoming more and more aware of the limitations of our world. Unless we want to condemn ourselves to slow suicide, we must not unscrupulously exhaust its reserves. We must not allow its biological cycles to be further poisoned. It is probably no coincidence that man today, after seeing his planet from the depths of space, is becoming aware of the material and biological condition of the inhabitants of this small 'spaceship' Earth.

In the foreword to the North-South Commission's report, there was talk of getting away from the "constant confusion" between growth and development. The priority was not the ever-increasing expansion of production, but a fair distribution of available income. Development in this sense means the unfolding of productive possibilities and human potential. In contrast to sustainable economic growth, which for most politicians and economic bosses, then as now, has been the primary objective of development, especially in poor countries, the demands of this report reflect the importance of human rights. It was already clear then that a neo-liberal policy geared solely to growth ultimately overruns people, not only by ruthlessly exploiting nature, but also by widening the gap between the few rich and the many poor, with all the consequences that entails. This was one of the topics closest to Margrit's heart!!

Encounter with Permaculture

An important event in Margrit's life was her first encounter, in 1981, with Bill Mollison and the idea of permaculture, which he had developed together with David Holmgren at the University of Hobart, Tasmania, Australia. Mollison visited the Kennedys as a guest in Berlin for a few weeks, giving them an unforgettable first introduction to the ideas and methods of permaculture. It proved to be a significant event in her life, not only due to her affinity for ecology, but as the first time that she had come across practical solutions with the potential to address the apparent conflict between ecology and the economy, driven by a need for continuous growth. Margrit and Declan also immediately began to implement some of the new ideas in their own garden.

❖ We had already been growing our own vegetables in Berlin, in our terraced house garden of six by twelve meters. For two years, we grew about forty percent of our food ourselves, with a minimum of work. We ate hardly any meat and fish, but instead lots of salad and wild herbs. There was a raised bed, thickly covered with hay mulch, in which I dug small furrows. Once in early summer, I pelleted (coated with rock flour) seeds and left it up to the weather and season to determine when they would germinate. I was amazed at how much yield can be achieved in such a small space. To this day, my favourite definition is: 'permaculture is a dance with nature, in which nature leads'. This kind of gardening – watching what grows, a little harvesting and a lot of mulching, especially where the wild herbs grow back too much – made me happy".

Margrit and Declan had twice visited Bill Mollison and David Holmgren in Australia, receiving their diplomas in permaculture design there. From 1982 on, they began an intensive search for a place where they could live a sustainable life, consistent with ecology and in accordance with the principles of permaculture.

- We have always agreed that we could only fully implement permaculture, with everything that goes with it – such as fruit and vegetable cultivation, animal husbandry, fish farming, low-energy houses, renewable energy systems, and the recycling of water and materials – as part of a larger group. Over a period of three years we travelled the world, from Germany to Greece to Australia, seeing countless projects, and it became clear that nobody was able to do it alone. We saw permaculture projects of such beauty that we were left speechless. Everywhere we went we considered: do we want to participate in this one? And everywhere something was wrong. In one project we were expected to go to church every Sunday. This was a group of Protestant Christians who would have liked to take us in. I also go to church. But I wouldn't have liked to do so out of obligation. In other projects, we felt as if one could cut the thick air of unresolved, interpersonal conflicts with a knife, and we were happy to get out again. The main problem was often that people thought it was already enough to have the same ecological goals – but didn't take into account the necessity for the resolution of human conflict in their work, so the relationships between the residents were soon literally eaten away by unresolved disputes."

Because of her work for the IBA, Margrit was often invited to give lectures at home and abroad, where she would present her experiences and ideas. She used model projects to show how energy could be saved, water consumption could be reduced, and urban districts made greener. However, despite all the enthusiasm of her audiences, she was repeatedly told that commitment to the environment does not *pay off.* The direct benefits were disputed, and the investment costs were criticized as being too high. The more this criticism was repeated, the more it became a key experience for Margrit.

❖ This began to annoy me. What did people mean by that, anyway: that it doesn't *pay off*? And what good would it do us if everything were to *pay off*, but we could no longer drink the water, hardly breathe the air, eat our food, or sleep because of all the noise? But I had begun to feel uncertain. Why was it so difficult to put all these good ideas into practice? I had to find out, or the solutions would never be sufficiently realizable. It was already clear to me that at this early stage, there weren't yet any large series. Nothing was mass produced; every ecological component was almost a one-off, in other words expensive. And the building regulations stood in the way; as did the financing guidelines, as well as people's habits. Architects still had little experience and didn't know how to design these details. In short: everywhere there were nothing but obstacles. But I also knew there was something else about the statement: *'It doesn't pay off'* that I hadn't quite understood."

The year 1982 brought a watershed moment. Declan was invited to speak at a conference on "Ecology and Economics," and Margrit accompanied him to the event, which took place on a farm in Lower Saxony.

❖ We arrived at the meeting place a half an hour late. It was a large hall in the middle of a market garden, with beds and greenhouses. We opened the door as quietly as possible. I will never forget the sight. We stood at the back of the hall, and in front of us was a sea of grey heads, at least eighty people, about half men and half women, and all of them grey to white-haired. 'What is this?' we silently asked ourselves. The new topic 'ecology and economics' and these old people... In our minds, it didn't go together at all. At first sight, we were just considering an orderly retreat, when the conference leader noticed us. Mr. S., who was just introducing the next speaker, saw us standing hesitantly at the back and said with pleasure: 'Here you are, there are still seats available here in the front.' All eighty participants turned around, and we marched along the line of curious glances to the front row. Apparently, we had only missed the preliminaries, because the first speaker was about to give his presentation: Helmut Creutz."

The Money Issue and the Financing of Ecological Projects

It was a turning point for Margrit, meeting this lively, warm and practical man who had just given up his profession as an architect to work exclusively as an economic analyst and publicist. Creutz explained in his lecture how interest and compound interest ultimately generate an exponential growth curve, and the consequences that result from this.

❖ I suddenly understood why the economy and ecology can never be united in this monetary system. It was as if a hundred pennies dropped at once. It was like a veil being lifted. I sat there as if struck by lightning. Had I found the missing link? Could compound interest be the unseen destructive mechanism in the world's gearbox? Could one small flaw in the design of our monetary system be responsible for everything from corporate bankruptcies to unemployment, environmental destruction and war? Was there really an irreconcilable contradiction between ecology and economics as a result of the exponential growth of money? In any case, I suddenly realized what people meant when they always said at the end of my ecology lectures that: *'It doesn't pay off'*. Plain and simple, it meant that the profits of such projects would not be able to compete with the current interest rates. Neither the interest demanded by the bank nor that which one would accrue if one were to put the money – instead of investing it in ecological projects – into a savings account."

As illuminating and comprehensive as Helmut Creutz's lecture had been, the contradiction continued to stir Margrit's thoughts. Should it be possible to pinpoint the cause of so many obvious problems down to a single fundamental flaw in the monetary system? Now she wanted to know for sure and took with her all the literature on the subject that had been laid out at the meeting.

❖ Back in Berlin, I spent every spare minute reading in the subway. In the breaks at work. In the evening, before falling asleep. In the morning, when I woke up before the alarm clock rang. For six months. And I always ended up at the same point: This Helmut Creutz is right. It's really is true: In our monetary system there is a small but significant error in the form of interest, which, with the resulting compound interest, makes the system grow exponentially, and which has caused war, crash and revolution ever since the interest-based monetary system has existed – that is, for about 5000 years."

Margrit began to tell friends and colleagues about it. Some of them shrugged their shoulders, others teased her that she had, no doubt, discovered a new and exciting topic for herself. But Margrit had gained a new perspective that she increasingly adopted, because she had immediately understood what it would mean if enough people recognized the error in the system and acted accordingly.

❖ I knew from sociological studies that it doesn't take all people in a society to change something, but only a certain percentage, and that – I thought -- one could achieve that with the right information. I still hadn't realized how solid the prison of thought is, when it comes to money. That took a while."

In the following years she developed a close co-operation with Helmut Creutz. She worked out an ever more precise knowledge of what Silvio Gesell called the "free economy" and also established intensive, friendship-based collaboration with other free economists.

***

In 1983, shortly after meeting Helmut Creutz, another important encounter took place, when Margrit met Hildur Jackson, who became a good friend of hers in the years that followed. They also met at a conference, this time at the Svanholm community farm in Denmark. Hildur Jackson and her husband Ross were particularly interested in, and committed to, supporting issues related to the environment, and also had financed ecological projects through their own foundation. When Bill Mollison asked Declan to help further spread permaculture, the Jacksons and their Gaia Foundation provided the initial funding for the project.

❖ For a long time, I was only able to gather hints about this foundation's funding source. Eventually I learned that Ross, with the support of financial experts, was using the cash profits from international currency speculation for ecological objectives. 'Ecologists don't understand much about money,' said Ross, 'but I know something about it. However, I can't take care of all the environmental stuff at the same time. So, working with the professionals I know, I raise the money to promote beneficial environmental projects.' What I didn't yet know was that a certain Bernard Lietaer was one of the leading financial experts behind this initiative."

***

Margrit's ended her work for the IBA in 1984. It had been an extremely successful experience, in part due to the record number of visitors to the events that focused on ecology. Margrit had made skillful use of her opportunities to organise events and had invited many renowned personalities to Berlin for lectures that received widespread attention. Now she was considering a visiting professorship for urban ecology at the Gesamthochschule (University) in Kassel, which she took up in the succeeding years. She also began the undertaking of an important new direction in her life, which initially began with a trip to Australia lasting several months.

❖ Declan and I both wanted to apply our knowledge of ecology and permaculture and were looking for a suitable place for a project. For a few months –

Declan had been given a research semester – we were in Australia. There were excellent conditions, equally interested people and projects, and a lot of cheap land. I was immediately offered an extremely exciting job there. The Ministry of Environment of the State of Victoria in Melbourne wanted me, as head of an innovation department, to carry out an ecological urban redevelopment in the western suburbs of Melbourne. It would involve a comparable task to what we had done at the IBA in Berlin under Hardt-Waltherr Hämer, in terms of 'cautious urban renewal'. The position was well equipped with money and staff. There was a lot of vacancy in the western suburbs of Melbourne at that time. Factories, where ammunition had been produced during World War II, had later been converted into huge meat processing plants, but were now empty due to the decline in meat consumption. Everyone reflected the social problems associated with vacancy."

In hindsight, it is remarkable when such specific opportunities as this seem to synchronistically recur in one's life, particularly when it occurs independent from the place.

At least, that's how Margrit saw it, because later – not in Australia, but somewhere completely different – she would be intensively involved with the conversion of a comparable site, that had been shaped by the production of armaments under adverse working conditions.

Lebensgarten Ecovillage

As of 1983, American Pershing II nuclear missiles were stationed in Germany as part of NATO's double-track decision (rearmament in conjunction with simultaneous disarmament negotiations). At the same time, German forests were dying at an alarming rate. So Margrit and Declan considered emigrating to Australia in order to create a model project based on the principles of permaculture. In their view, actions were far more effective than a thousand words.

Margrit had also spoken about this on New Year's Eve 1984 in a last telephone conversation with her father, who explicitly encouraged her to put this idea into practice. A little later, in March 1985, while the Kennedys were still "Down Under", he died, and her brother Reinhard took over the management of the company. And then, after Margrit and Declan had returned to Germany, finally found exactly what they had been looking for – through what seemed an extraordinary set of circumstances!

❖ One night at one o'clock there was a knock at our hall door. I said, 'Declan, someone's knocking.' He answered, 'You're crazy, it's already one in the morning!' I said, 'No, I'm not crazy; someone's knocking.' I open the front door and see a sympathetic, blond curly-haired young man in front of me. He silently hands me a letter from a doctor friend, who knew that we were looking for a location for our permaculture project. In the letter, she recommended that we examine this possibility, which this young man named Christian Benzin was offering. I invited him in, and we talked to him until three in the morning. Christian had bought a site in Lower Saxony, a settlement with sixty-five houses and a large complex of buildings in the middle, which had been built by the Nazis before the war. He first wanted to sell or rent these houses, as weekend homes. But then he was invited to Findhorn and was so impressed by the community that he decided against the originally planned commercial use, and in favour of building a German 'Findhorn Community'. Instead he was now looking for people to join this community. His three main goals for building and renewing the community were Peace instead of war, tolerance instead of intolerance and creativity instead of obedience. After half an hour I knew: This is it! The following weekend there was to be a first on-site meeting. Declan had an appointment elsewhere, so I went alone. There were eighty people there. And when I saw the place and the people, I immediately thought, 'Yeah, this is the place we've been looking for the past three years.' I saw the potential of the large building in the middle, where the community activities and seminar operations take place today. And I saw the sixty-five settlement buildings. It was immediately clear to me that we would not have to live in caravans, as was still the case in Findhorn at that time. I had looked at two of these houses, which we later bought, on the very first day. I decided to stay in Germany, where I was born and felt that I belonged and was responsible for what was happening. Declan made his approval conditional upon whether or not we would get a piece of land on which to plant trees. He'd been having the same dream for months. Every morning he'd wake up and say, "I've been planting trees all night again. And I knew that if he couldn't do that soon, he would become ill. Consequently, we went to Steyerberg together again. After we had both gone for a long walk around the grounds with friends – each of us with a different one – and come back, we said almost simultaneously: 'I've found the right property!' We compared the locations and discovered that we had found the same spot. By a stroke of luck, this property was also up for sale. And after some back and forth with the neighbouring farmer, who was also interested in it to round out his fields, we were actually able to buy it. In the end, the farmer was offered a better piece of land by the municipality because they wanted to support our project."

In October 1985 the time had arrived, and indeed, Margrit and Declan moved to Lebensgarten in Steyerberg. Everything was still rather improvised and the renovation of the houses, which had been empty for a long time and were accordingly run-down, was quite costly. But little by little a paradise was created – not only in the private rooms of the Kennedys – but on the whole area of the settlement. Margrit was happy and glad that she was now able to realize her ideas of an ecologically conscious life in full.

❖ It has always bothered me that people see ecology primarily as a concept of reduction: Using less water, less energy, less material, producing less waste, less this and less that. And at the end you ask yourself: 'Am I still allowed to live and breathe?' My idea, on the other hand, is that ecology must be a concept that reflects happiness, adventure, freedom and beauty. So that people come and say: 'This is so beautiful; I want that too'. That's why we had decided to create something that would inspire people. Our permaculture lean-to greenhouse has to be so beautiful that it inspires people and that they want it, instead of gold-plated plumbing fixtures and a whirlpool tub in their bathroom. It not only makes sense because one can grow food crops there without pesticides, or due to the energy savings, or the living space it adds in autumn and spring. It could even play a role in a survival strategy in case of emergency, since edible plants can be grown in it".

***

Their decision to move to an ecovillage was a very deliberate one. While concerned with the external aspects of a conscious, mindful life, it was also important to Margrit and Declan that there be opportunities for inner work on themselves. A life in community, supported by a liberating spiritual attitude that would flourish through cooperation with their neighbors was a matter of great significance to them. For this reason, they abandoned their career paths, which they could well have continued. This serious decision was not without controversy among their peers – many friends and acquaintances expressed their incomprehension to Margrit and Declan – but from the Kennedys' point of view, the decision was entirely consistent with their ideals and already long overdue.

❖ I was forty-five, Declan fifty-one, when we took this leap. We had great jobs and great career prospects! Our house in Berlin was almost paid off. Declan could have stayed at the university until retirement and I might have ended up in a high position at the Building Commission at some point. But it was clear to us: We can't always just talk about it, we have to implement this permaculture concept somewhere. Only later did it become clear to us how risky such a collaborative project actually is; how many such projects have gone wrong over time. And yet, to this day, we are certain that it was the best decision we ever made! Of course, I expected that I would regret it at some point. As we sat in Berlin and struggled to decide, we thought there would surely be hours when we would say to ourselves: Gee, if only we had stayed in the city. But that hasn't happened to us, even in all these years."

In Lebensgarten, Margrit and Declan were introduced to Non-Violent Communication (NVC), a method developed in the mid-1980s by the American psychologist Marshall Bertram Rosenberg. The main point of NVC, is that communication should be characterised by a more appreciative attitude towards each other, which enables and supports cooperation and creativity. Rosenberg, who received his doctorate in clinical psychology from the University of Wisconsin-Madison, developed his ideas and the concept of NVC in light of his involvement with the American civil rights movement. After the method had proven its worth in peacefully overcoming racial segregation in schools and other public institutions, NVC became increasingly widespread – even in arenas where, as in Lebensgarten, the aim is a generally peaceful, cooperative communal life.

Margrit began a concerted effort to work on self-awareness and her own personality in Lebensgarten. Her very strong-willed, at times choleric personality became much calmer – although this occasionally required an unprecedented degree of patience on her part. But the effort was worthwhile, because change did take place.

❖ The first five years in Steyerberg I was often ill because I had to examine all the shadow aspects of my personality. In the community, Declan and I were the perfect projection surfaces for all problems with parents, with teachers, with money, with titles – and also with having achieved something in life. We had to do a tremendous amount of work, on ourselves, with our shadow sides and with others, to come through that situation. Because as long as the projections resonated with us, we were trapped in conflict. After almost exactly five years I knew: now it's finished. The projections stopped resonating. And I noticed how they no longer affected me, and after some time the other residents looked for some other projection screen. But until we got that far, it was sometimes very hard. Even if you think you know and understand a person through and through, sooner or later you always come to a point where you think: 'Oh, that's who he is! I never saw him or her that way.' This is part of the social training in Lebensgarten: I've learned to appreciate the things that go well, and to emphasize those things that are going very well. And if something isn't going well, to observe it without giving it any particular weight. To take everything a little easier. You just have to develop the sun in your heart when – and this is just the way it is, here in Northern Germany – it's sometimes missing on the outside."

***

Margrit and Declan were complementary in many ways, perhaps because they were so different in their styles of expression. While Margrit's verbal presentation was rather dry and clearly structured, Declan's speech was mostly spontaneous and moved in a dance-like way. Margrit worked out some passages of her lectures down to the last detail of the wording, Declan usually had faith in the moment and his spontaneous intuition. Whenever possible, they would listen to each other and then give each other helpful feedback.

- We give each other wonderful feedback, and also support each other in our issues and through our activities. It's true that without each other, we would never have gotten where we are today. I have rarely seen two people each have a career and support each other. We have always been incredibly important to each other. Actually, I usually take the 'male' role in our relationship, and Declan takes the 'female' role – supportive and in the background."

Whenever Margrit was invited to give lectures, she not only thoroughly prepared herself, but also looked for ways to understand as precisely as possible who she was dealing with. This made it possible for her to truly reach her audience. She often started her seminars, which lasted several hours, by gathering questions and letting everyone in the room have their say. Sometimes she then worked with constellations to make the less conscious relationships to the subject more tangible. And the lecture would come only at the very end, in which she would then incorporate what she had previously presented.

One of Margrit's particular strengths was her ability to quickly grasp ideas and transfer them into a conceptual framework. She was not only familiar with the theoretical side of things, but also with the very practical tasks of everyday life. In addition to her skill in handling the many moves, conversions and renovations, she was adept at heavy physical work with a spade in her hand. The Kennedys had been able to start their permaculture project in Lebensgarten. Now, countless – indeed thousands of trees were planted, in order to transform parts of the predominantly coniferous forest into a mixed forest.

- We planned and built, dug and planted. Everything was new and exciting, full of challenges and learning processes. I was quite pleased with our decision."

A New Field of Work

Among the many special attributes of Margrit's life, a defining one stands out – that she, as an architect, increasingly took on the issue of money. Her encounters with permaculture and Helmut Creutz had made it completely clear why it was so difficult to be committed to ecological principles in the context of the prevailing economy. Since then, she had spent more and more time presenting the problem and showing possible solutions. In the first years, such explanations were incorporated into her projects, lectures, workshops and consultations. Later, they became the focus.

On her way to becoming an internationally known money expert, an encounter in Cologne in August 1986 with a spiritual teacher who was a descendant of Native Americans marked a defining moment. On the advice of a friend, Margrit had registered for one of his seminars, signing up for both the introductory basic course, as well as the advanced course, held immediately afterwards. During this course, something extraordinary occurred while in meditation: suddenly, Margrit saw herself giving a lecture on the issue of money at the United Nations.

- I saw myself standing at the lectern in this round room in the UN building and making a plea for the reform of our monetary system. But in my mind, I was reluctant to go so deeply into the monetary issue. Then something happened that is said to happen at the moment of our death: my whole life flashed past my inner eye in seconds. I saw every detail with absolute clarity. At that moment I realized that everything I had ever done - all the subjects and all the journeys, all the titles and degrees, all the disappointments and mistakes, all the encounters and struggles - everything I had experienced had prepared me for this task. It was suddenly clear to me: with regard to this subject, all the paths and detours of my life suddenly made sense. 'Well,' I reluctantly rather than happily agreed, saying almost grudgingly: 'I'll do it.' I knew there was no alternative for me."

After the seminar Margrit went to Kassel, where she stayed overnight at her brother's apartment. He was out of town and had left the key with her. No sooner had she laid down when it occurred to her that a book, and the questions about money that this book must address, had to be written. Despite her fatigue, she immediately began making notes, and by 3:00 a.m., she had finally outlined the entire concept. She'd even sketched out the cover design, with the earth in the middle, surrounded by eight figures. But that was not all...

❖ I woke up at 9:00 a.m., and at about 10:00 a.m. I called Declan: 'You won't believe what ...'. He immediately interrupted me, saying: 'Tell me about this later. A woman from Australia called. She wants to invite you to a lecture. It's six o'clock at night right now, and she's only in the office for half an hour.' So, I spoke to this woman on the phone, who had heard my lecture on permaculture in Adelaide a few months earlier. She said, 'We'd like you to be the keynote speaker for the opening address at two conferences in November 1986, in Melbourne and Sydney, which we're currently organizing in cooperation with the United Nations.' I couldn't believe my ears. It had been just fifteen hours since, in meditation, I had seen myself speaking before the United Nations, and here I was invited to be the keynote speaker at two UN conferences. Yet these talks were not intended to be about money, but about cooperative housing. I requested some time to think about it, and then I considered all of it. How could I reconcile the experiences of the past few days and last night with this request? Then it was suddenly clear: I would accept the invitation if I could talk about cooperative money instead of the building of cooperative housing. Because if we had that, everything else would be cooperative anyway. When one considers how much compound interest is included in the cost of housing, and similarly in rental costs, then it's already evident that cooperation or helping each other in the building of a house can bypass the need to pay interest. But if the currency system were to be changed to complementary, then everything, not just housing and habitation, but everything else necessary for living could be made 'co-operative'. And it was my intention to reveal just this. I resolutely picked up the phone again. 'Okay', said the conference manager, 'If you can link your topic in any way to cooperative housing, then you can talk about whatever you want.' For a long while I sat quietly in the leather armchair next to the telephone, listening to the clock in the kitchen ticking, the traffic outside rushing by, and tried to understand what was going on in my life."

Shortly after giving her presentation at the two UN conferences in Australia, Margrit was invited to Norway for the 2nd. UN Women's Conference to discuss the issue of money. This conference took place in mid-August 1987.

❖ My plenary address there – immediately after Prime Minister Gro Brundtland – was really, really good."

Norway's Prime Minister at the time, Gro Harlem Brundtland – born the same year as Margrit – pursued a policy that Margrit could identify with very well. She filled eight of the 18 ministerial posts with women, a fact that had received widespread international attention. Margrit had also been delighted by the 1987 report "Our Common Future" by the United Nations World Commission on Environment and Development, chaired by Gro Harlem Brundtland.

❖ In the meantime, I had a very special relationship with Norway. Over the previous ten years, there had been many occasions for me to participate in events and give lectures on the topics of women and architecture, urban ecology and monetary and land reform. Whether it was about women and architecture, ecology and permaculture or money, I was almost better known in Scandinavia than in Germany. I loved the people in Scandinavia – and they loved me."

***

1987 was a particularly memorable year for Margrit, as she concentrated largely on working at the permaculture site in Lebensgarten. Instead of traveling far afield for lectures and workshops, she and Declan together planted more than six thousand bushes and trees. Following their custom, the Kennedys also spent four weeks vacationing on Hydra. It had to be four weeks for real calm and relaxation to set in, allowing Margrit the peace to write the book she'd outlined after the seminar in Cologne. The first three weeks on the Greek island passed without much activity.

❖ Then, quite unexpectedly, after breakfast on Monday morning, I had an idea for the money book. I sat down at my desk. When the church clock rang, I looked up. It was already noon. I made lunch, sat down again to finish my notes. I looked at the clock – and it was time for dinner. That's when I realized something was going on. I worked twelve hours – from ten o'clock in the morning to ten o'clock in the evening – and had more energy afterwards than when I'd started working. The second night Declan was angry. He noticed me writing non-stop and enjoying it. He complained, 'We've only got a few days' holiday left and you're always working!' We argued until one in the morning, when I said, 'Declan, let's stop and go to bed. We're not going to solve anything now. Tomorrow's another day.' The next morning, I woke up to his laughter. 'What is there to laugh about?' I asked. 'I had a dream,' he said. We were trained in dream interpretation. However, we would have understood this dream without any training: *I'm running from Declan, uphill, my arms loaded with parcels. At some point I start dropping one package after another. He picks them all up. As he does so, he gets madder and madder and madder. Finally, he'd had enough; he sits down on a stone by the wayside and opens the parcels. Inside are his socks, his undershirts, his ties...* From that moment on, he was wonderfully tolerant of my work."

During the last days of her vacation, which Margrit experienced as being in a state of "perfect presence", the book was composed out of a continuous stream of thought. The text, which she wanted to have ready before she spoke at the conference in Norway, was written in English. She had deliberately chosen to do this in order to express her thoughts as simply and as comprehensibly as possible, to every reader. Finally, she was finished and was able to enjoy an unforgettable last vacation day with Declan, who had meanwhile created the graphics for the book. Back in Steyerberg, she spent two more weeks putting the finishing touches on the manuscript.

❖ Suddenly my eyes fell on a permaculture magazine in the bookshelf next to my desk, which had arrived from Australia a few days before. On the cover was that famous photo of the earth that the astronauts had taken from space: the image of the little blue planet in a dark universe, with a few stars visible in the distance. So, a photo and not a drawing! Well, I thought, maybe that would work. Taking the magazine, I put my tracing paper with the sketch from the cover of the book on top of it and was instantly thunderstruck. The contour of my globe matched the picture exactly to the millimetre. It looked wonderful. At that moment, for the first time in my life, I heard the angels laughing. They were practically holding their bellies with laughter: 'She always assumes she can sort everything out with her mind', they giggled, 'we've shown her who's really in charge here.' Yes, they had. I've never really been more amazed in all my life."

When everything was finally completed, it was already four o'clock in the morning. She and Declan celebrated in their own style, joyfully dancing a Viennese waltz.

In the following years, the book "Interest and Inflation Free Money – How to Create an Exchange Medium that Works for Everybody", was continually expanded in terms of content, translated into 22 languages, and eventually spread all across the world. Can be downloaded from her website: margritkennedy.de

Since the Kennedys have always had an extensive network, it was not surprising that an increasing number of their friends and acquaintances took an interest in the money issue. This led to the decision to organize dedicated conferences in Lebensgarten, which were held starting in 1990. The ecovillage's infrastructure was ideal for this purpose, and so more and more people gathered once a year to spend a few days exploring the theme of money, learning about projects and coordinating joint activities. For this purpose, the framework of the meetings was always designed in such a way that the ideas and projects of those present could be acknowledged. The aim was to create connections and facilitate good networking opportunities. Due to the conferences' international flavor, they were held alternately in German and English.

***

Margrit had become friends with Hildur Jackson and was in regular contact with her. Hildur, a lawyer who had a deep interest in ecological issues, had of course also read Margrit's book on the subject of money. And because she was so impressed by it, she had soon passed it on to a man who had been responsible for the

"GAIA Hedge Fund" in the Cayman Islands for several years. She wanted to know what this manager thought of Margrit's presentation. It was in this way that Hildur Jackson first introduced Margrit and Bernard Lietaer to each other.

- A few weeks later Bernard called from the Cayman Islands: the epicenter of currency speculation. He thanked me, congratulated me on the book and was very pleased with the solution proposed in it: 'For fifteen years I have been trying to find a solution to the exponential growth in the monetary system. I have not succeeded. I found it in your book,' he literally said, because I will never forget that sentence. As Hildur considered him the person who knew the most about money in the world, and because I trusted her judgement, his call ended nine years of uncertainty for me. For the first time, I had the feeling: 'It's not me who's crazy; it's the world that's crazy to tolerate such a destructive system'."

The significance of Margrit's and Bernard Lietaer's introduction to one another should not be underestimated. Already in his first telephone conversation with Margrit herself, Lietaer expressed that, thanks to her, he had come to understand the fact that growth driven by interest and compound interest creates problems in the monetary system. This was a turning point for him, a man renowned in the official world of finance, as from that point on, until the end of his life he advocated for a radically different, ecological understanding of the monetary system, with all his professional competence. Margrit therefore provided an important stimulus for Lietaer, given that his life's work, which is considerable in content and scope, was largely devoted to alternatives to the prevailing monetary system.

Professorship in Hanover

Margrit was always concerned that women and men should have equal rights in their professional and social lives. She vehemently rejected the traditional understanding of gender roles, with which she had been brought up. In the early 1990s, when she was offered a professorship for building technology and resource-saving construction at the Architecture department of the University of Hanover, she personally encountered this again, indicating the fact that not much had changed in terms of equality in the academic world.

Margrit wasn't expecting such an offer, particularly as she had already been turned down a few times in previous years for similar positions. And even at this juncture, her name wasn't first on the list of proposed candidates. But unlike the other applicants, all of whom were male, she had a doctorate.

❖ Usually, one isn't appointed if they're name appears second on the list. But in Lower Saxony, the SPD had just won the state elections and had reached an agreement with the Greens to promote women to leading positions. Helga Schuchardt became Minister of Science and Culture and the list of nominees came across her desk. 'How typical, a woman in second place', she said, 'let's have a look here.' As she later told me, she called five well-known architects and asked: 'Do you know an architect named Margrit Kennedy?' All five of them reacted positively, and as a result she appointed me from second place to the professorship."

Margrit accepted the appointment and soon noticed how this new position affected her reputation in the eyes of many people. The academic title *Professor* brought her far more attention, even when she wasn't talking about architecture, but about money. However, it wasn't initially easy for her to live up to the new position in all respects. She was already quite familiar with resource-saving construction – primarily due to her experience in connection with the IBA – but not with the requirements in the field of building technology. The technical details of energy, water and electricity supply, wastewater and the recycling of valuable materials were still little known to her. And there were constantly new developments to which she had to respond. The only way to remedy this was to put in more hours than she had expected. Almost every weekend she was busy preparing her courses. In the process, she now knew very well what worked well and what didn't. She lived under this relatively constant tension all of the time until her retirement, which she herself requested eleven years later. In the meantime, however, she kept abreast of new developments in a field very close to her heart.

❖ What was really positive and encouraging during these eleven years of professorship was that I was able to see how the ecological ideas that I had helped to develop in the early eighties as part of the IBA were slowly infiltrating architectural studies. Many people had now realised that the level of resource consumption in construction and building processes could not continue in the same way. And by the time I left the university, the breakthrough with ecological building had practically been achieved. Virtually everything we had called for in the early 1980s was now state of the art."

Other Money

It was in the same year that she was appointed as professor at the University of Hanover, that Margrit became aware of Bernard Lietaer, with whom she would share extensive exchanges on the topic of money in the decades to come. Thus, she also took part – at first from a distance, as a first personal meeting came about only a few years later – in how Lietaer developed his ideas of what he called a "complementary currency". According to Lietaer, it was necessary for the monetary system, and the predominant way of doing business, to be supplemented by currencies created independently of the state. In this way, "monetary ecosystems" (this term is found again and again in Lietaer's work) would be created, which would supplement those currencies characterized as "male", with "female" characteristics.

This approach of bringing particularly female characteristics into monetary and economic processes was perfectly in line with Margrit's ideas. The emergence and growth of a movement for new types and systems of currency to be introduced from the bottom up corresponded much more closely with her life experience than the idea of potential change initiated by political bodies, in a top-down manner. But this did not correspond with Helmut Creutz's ideas, nor to the Free-Thinking Economists, associated with him, for whom Margrit also felt an affinity. In other words, a degree of conflict was inevitable.

- Helmut Creutz thought – perhaps rightly – that regional currencies would be nothing more than a crutch. The mini currency experiments, he believed, would either be irrelevant or if they were successful, prohibited. You can only take a few steps in the right direction on a steamship heading in the wrong direction, he wrote in an article in the *'Zeitschrift für Sozialökonomie'* (Journal for Social Economics). It is still crucial to change the direction – that is, to change the monetary system on a large scale, and from above. We were nevertheless united by the conviction that an understanding of monetary interrelationships is the absolute prerequisite for a broader citizens' movement which, similar to the environmental and anti-nuclear movements, is

> striving for a turnaround in money parallel to the agricultural and energy turnaround, and is moving towards the great goal of changing the monetary structures in many small steps."

Margrit and Declan Kennedy occupy a special place among those of their generation who have successfully championed ecological and life-enhancing issues that benefit the whole of society. By the 1990s, they were already public figures whose expertise was widely recognized and valued. Margrit was always on the road, giving lectures and workshops, doing interviews for various media. Yet she knew only too well, due to her many, sometimes painful experiences, that some things take a long time to materialize.

Margrit experienced this tension of having understood a lot of the good without being able to trigger a rapid spread of the corresponding models of action – as a special burden she had to bear. When she told her friend Gisela Reinicke how difficult it was for her to integrate the inspiration and experiences she'd garnered from Lebensgarten into her work at the University of Hanover, she was relieved to hear her friend's comment that her claim was tantamount to squaring the circle – that it would never be entirely possible to achieve.

❖ At that moment, I felt a huge weight fall from my shoulders. With these simple words, Gisela released me from a sense of personal responsibility, the enormity of which was threatening to make me ill.

Her comment helped me to let it go, and I went back to work strengthened and liberated."

***

The multi-volume book "Future-oriented Ecological Housing Development in Europe", was published in 1993, while, "Interest and Inflation Free Money" enjoyed ever wider distribution throughout the 1990s. Many translations were produced during this period, as there were people who were actively committed to having it published in the relevant languages. Declan took care of coordinating the translation work as well as contact with the publishers. He had also added a separate unit on the subject of money to his permaculture courses. In this way, everyone who, out of ecological conviction, had signed up for the permaculture design course was reached directly.

Margrit and Declan managed a huge amount of work, but they were also extremely happy that so much was in motion, and now came together in a meaningful way. There was a component of this kind of experience that had to do with their worldview, whereby meaningful events sometimes occur precisely when the direct will is not directly involved in what is happening. Margrit wrote about this to her granddaughter:

❖ Dear Nora, if you should ask me 'what is the most important contribution you could make in this world', it is *the practice of positive thinking*. As there is nothing that happens in this world that has not first been imagined, it is better to give space to positive changes in our thinking rather than negative and destructive thoughts. This is an important contribution, because it's something you can do that sets yourself and this world on the right path. It is terribly easy to give in to feelings of sadness and anger when one sees how some things develop. It is a bit harder to orient oneself to the positive aspects that also exist in the world and to support them as much as possible. If we can see ourselves as a part of the whole body of humanity, we are individually as important as every cell in our body, and like them, we can make our fully autonomous contribution to the whole. We can see ourselves as individuals who have something unique to offer this world. For this we have to find out what makes us unique and to develop it. We can also use it to help others to make their own unique contribution, and to pave the way for truly fruitful cooperation in all areas of life. But most importantly, it seems to me, is that we ourselves take responsibility for what happens in the area we can influence. That is what I would like to see."

And to illustrate in detail what she meant by this she mentioned an incident that occurred while on holiday on La Palma in April 1993.

❖ Declan and I had been on a long mountain hike and had enjoyed a lengthy rest at the top of a high mountain ledge overlooking a view of the sea. On the way back down, we had almost arrived at the rental car we had parked in a parking lot halfway up the mountain, when I realized that I had left my glasses up on the cliff. I was really annoyed at myself for being so scatterbrained. But Declan simply said, 'Who knows what the real purpose is?', and so we went all the way up the mountain again, this time by car, over hill and dale. It was a dirt road. We found the glasses and were just about to drive on, when around a bend a big heavy-set man approached us. When we took a closer look, he was wearing slippers and was groping his way with a cane for the blind. Braking, Declan stopped the car and I got out and walked towards the man. I didn't know what language he spoke, but I asked, 'Can we help you?' He answered in German and it turned out he was from Frankfurt – and blind. He had been wandering around since eleven o'clock in the morning and was at his wits' end. All he wanted to know was: 'How do I get to that village down there?' He'd heard the sounds, the voices of the people echoing from below, and it had sounded pretty close. But to get there, he would have had to walk for miles; the path paralleled the mountain in long descending curves. He would definitely have been on the road for another three or four hours. And it was already getting quite chilly and increasingly dark. So, we asked him if he would like to come with us. The car we had rented was quite small. I got in the back and let the man have the front passenger seat. Declan tried to drive off, but the car didn't move. The road was too steep, and because the car was rear-wheel drive, the wheels just spun. So, we asked the man to sit in the backseat. It wasn't easy with his mass, and the car, of course, only had two doors. But, finally, it worked. Then this man told us quite cheerfully that he has had such experiences time and again, and that these situations had often been quite perilous for him. But that one way or another, he was always rescued. Apparently, he needed the occasional thrill of putting his life in danger. Maybe he found his life as a blind person too boring... He had completely relied on the fact that someone would pick him up, taking it for granted that we would come his way. Anyway, we now knew why I had left my glasses on the cliff."

***

The need to be conscious of the physical and mental well-being of the community and social life, as well as that of the human being, was absolutely clear to Margrit. It's possible for the "social organism" to be healthy or sick. Therefore, it requires just as much conscious attention as the human body. It was in this context that she found her way to the ideas of Dr. Max Otto Bruker, who had made a name for himself as a non-fiction author, doctor and politician. Margrit met him during a stay at his Lahnstein Clinic, where at the time he worked as the medical director. The two remained friends ever since.

Dr. Bruker, who was regarded as a representative of naturopathy, had particular insight with regard to the vitality of vegetables cultivated with care, as a part of the wholefood diet he advocated. This soon led to many points of convergence with permaculture, but also with

Margrit's ideas concerning the necessary creation of a healthy monetary system. At one point, Margrit gave a lecture on these ideas at the Lahnstein Clinic, which was attended by nearly a thousand mostly health-care professionals. The response was impressive!

❖ Early on, Dr. Bruker had the insight that a 'sick' monetary system ultimately makes people sick too, and that what is needed is a system that serves the common good rather than greed. A number of health professionals who heard my lecture in Lahnstein took copies of my book with them and sold them at their own events. That's how it soon became well known in Germany."

Margrit was also able to pursue this idea – of creating healthy, social conditions with complementary currencies – when she and Declan were invited by Hildur and Ross Jackson to help shape the goals of the GAIA Foundation.

❖ Before distributing funds for ecological projects for the first time in 1993, Hildur and Ross had come to Steyerberg for a weekend. They wanted to discuss with us which projects could be eligible for funding. I saw then, after my years of experience with the beginnings of ecological construction and permaculture, that most ecological approaches were too technical and linear: saving energy, saving water, reducing waste, noise abatement, greening, air quality improvement. For each of these building blocks the latest developments and techniques had to be financed. But there was no funding for holistic approaches that would bring all these aspects together, or the attempt to combine them with social considerations, such as our own Lebensgarten Steyerberg project, among others. Hildur and Ross understood this immediately: 'What if we were to call these experiments *eco-villages* and promote them?' This weekend the ecovillage network was initiated not only for Germany and Europe, but worldwide. This later became the 'Global Ecovillage Network' (GEN), which has now also become a worldwide non-governmental organization (NGO) recognized by the UN."

As helpful as this financial contribution was for the establishment of the Ecovillage Network and later GEN, some of the parties involved nevertheless found it contradictory that money gained from speculative financial transactions was being used to support ecological projects. Aimed at making maximum profit as quickly as possible, the speculative handling of money stands in stark contrast to an ecologically and socially meaningful economy. And here, a conflict that had emerged for some during this time was pacified, but never fully resolved.

***

A joyful event in Margrit's personal life took place in 1994 with the birth of her granddaughter, Nora. After ten years of partnership, Antja had married Bernd Oberländer in 1993. Margrit spontaneously travelled to Berlin to support the young family in the very practical aspects of the household. She would do this later time and again, devoting great attention to lovingly nurture the family ties, despite her many professional commitments. On weekends, Margrit and Declan stepped in as babysitters, so that the young parents could relax undisturbed.

Over the years, a particularly affectionate relationship developed between the grandmother and the growing granddaughter. They travelled together to many European cities and spent winter holidays in the mountains. At times, Margrit's views could be quite unconventional, for example when she once suggested taking her granddaughter out of school to attend a convention, she reasoned that the young girl would certainly learn more there than at school!

***

It was an important part of Margrit's life to be involved with and participate in international conferences and conventions. Since 1975, the UN's World Conferences of Women had been held in Mexico, Copenhagen and Nairobi and in 1995, Margrit was invited as a speaker to another such event, which took place in Beijing. The UN Women's Section, through which international standards are formulated, is committed to gender equality and women's rights worldwide. At the fourth UN Women's Conference in Beijing, twelve main problem areas, requiring specific action, were identified, including "women and poverty", "women in the economy", "women in power and decision-making positions" and "women and the environment".

All addressed issues that were of central importance to Margrit.

After attending the conference in Beijing, Margrit went to Norway, Argentina and Scotland, where she gave a talk for a conference at the Findhorn ecovillage. This community had been founded in 1962 by the couple Caddy and Dorothy MacLean. There, Margrit met Robert Meyer, who for over 40 years had served as personal advisor to all the General Secretaries of the UN, and who had also helped in the foundation of the Peace University in Costa Rica. An exchange then developed with Robert Meyer – who was studying complementary currencies through the books of Bernard Lietaer, particularly about the introduction of a currency with a guaranteed circulation mechanism, for eastern Europe.

Yet another important encounter with someone connected to the United Nations came about in New York in the late 1990s, when Declan met Helga Heineken. Her husband, a UN inspector, was one of those responsible for the investigation of Iraq's nuclear program.

❖ It was 1998. After an event at the United Nations in New York, Declan was on a bus to the airport. As the bus was about to leave, Helga Heineken, who spoke very little English and therefore had difficulty communicating with the bus driver, got on. Declan offered to translate and learned that she did not have enough cash to pay for the transfer to the airport. With his help the small problem was solved. As is customary in the UN, business cards were exchanged. When Helga read the name Declan Kennedy she said: 'That's strange. For years I have been trying to contact a woman named Margrit Kennedy in Germany. I would like to translate her book on urban ecology into Spanish. Perhaps you know each other?' Declan replied that he not only knew this woman but had been married to her for over 35 years. By the time they arrived at the airport, Declan had not only convinced Helga Heineken to translate the money book rather than the ecology book, but they had also agreed that the Spanish version should be published in about six months. And that is exactly what happened. Without this Spanish version of my book, I certainly would not have had the important experience with the Argentinian Credito that was so crucial to the later development of the regional money idea in Germany".

***

After making a trip to the northern Italian ecovillages in 1999, the Kennedys attended a conference in Alpbach, Austria, organized by Peter König and Veronica Spielbichler, to allow them the opportunity to share the idea of complementary currencies. Among the participants were Bernard Lietaer and his then partner Jacqui Dunne from the USA (originally from Ireland). Margrit was quite excited in advance of this first in-person encounter with Lietaer, with whom she'd been engaged in a dialogue on the subject for years.

Now each heard the other's lecture, then taking part in a lively discussion, which was enhanced by a visit to the museum of local history in Wörgl. It was in Wörgl in the 1930s that Michael Unterguggenberger – a former locomotive driver, then mayor – had undertaken his free money experiment, thus helping to offset the huge consequences of the world economic crisis for his small community. Both Bernard Lietaer and Margrit Kennedy frequently referred to Unterguggenberger's successes. Here in the museum they learned of "the Europa", which was conceived in the 1930s as a currency for European domestic trade.

The Europa currency was based on a shopping basket concept and was intended to replace the single common-denominator currency, as we have today, since giving up a gold-backed currency. Lietaer was working intensely on this idea, with his promotion of the Terra reference currency, with which other national currencies could be aligned.

The encounter between Margrit and Bernard Lietaer in Austria deepened their friendship and concluded with Margrit and Declan extending a warm invitation to Lietaer to visit them in Lebensgarten. It was not long before Lietaer accepted this invitation, arriving at the ecovillage in Lower Saxony for a working holiday of several months. Lietaer had nearly completed a major work on his ideas, but it had turned out to be extremely comprehensive, so the publisher had asked Margrit to read and shorten it where possible – a project that pushed Margrit to her limits, and brought Lietaer to Steyerberg for the first time!

- For each place where I could shorten, I found three others where I felt a sentence needed to be inserted. When I finished, the volume of the manuscript had not increased, but it had not decreased either. 'I simply cannot shorten it', I capitulated at my first meeting with the publisher. Declan suggested an idea and Mr. Riemann pragmatically accepted it: 'Then we'll just have to make two books out of it, because the German translation will lengthen it by further twenty percent or so.' When it became clear that the original manuscript would have to be divided into two books, Lietaer accepted our open invitation and came to Steyerberg for three months. We had many wonderful, long and enlightening conversations during these weeks about money and archetypes, about the world in general and money in particular. Once a week, Lietaer took us out to good restaurants for a spectacular dinner with the best wine and first-class food, to thank us for the accommodations. On those evenings, our discussions often had a special depth to them."

Lietaer and the Kennedys had become very close during this time, so even very personal matters and experiences were discussed. Thus, Lietaer spoke with the Kennedys about a conflict that had arisen with Ross Jackson, at the end of his work for the GAIA Fund.

At the end of the 1960s, Lietaer had developed an algorithm that enabled him to compute exchange-rate fluctuations for a wide variety of currencies, to make forecasts for the future. With this ingenious idea, he had worked as a consultant for a leading management consultancy in the USA at the time, then in various companies in different countries around the world. Business Week had named Lietaer the world's best fund manager of the year in 1991. So, he was already an internationally recognized expert when Ross Jackson recruited him for his GAIA Trust.

The agreement was that from the Cayman Islands, Lietaer would make a profit of several million dollars for the trust, which would then be used for ecological projects. Lietaer was to be involved in the decision as to which projects the money would fund. But things turned out differently.

When the profit target was actually reached, Ross Jackson expected Lietaer to generate further profits, and contrary to the agreement, he did not include him in the decision on the use of the money. So Lietaer and Jackson had ultimately parted ways on bad terms.

As friends of both Bernard Lietaer and Ross Jackson, the Kennedy's launched an attempt at mediation, organizing discussions which at any rate reduced the sharpness of the conflict. However, it could not be completely resolved.

***

By the turn of the millennium, Margrit had become widely known not only as an ecological architect, but also as a "money expert". But unlike her work as an architect, which had involved many practical projects in addition to research and teaching over the years, her commitment to complementary currencies lacked the practical experience of normal everyday life.

During one of her vacations in Greece in September 2000, this suddenly became clear to her. She realized that this was what had distressed her so much over the years, namely that, in terms of money reform, "nothing really progressed" in her understanding. She ultimately wanted truly practical examples in this field as well.

- Here Declan and I were again on the same wavelength, because he also always found it frustrating that neither of us could give a really satisfying answer when people would ask us after a money lecture: 'And what practical steps could we take now?' Giving the answer: 'Inform yourself, so that you can inform others' was no longer enough for us."

A theory without practice was not of much interest to Margrit. This concern, to enable the practical application of good ideas, had led the Kennedys to move to Lebensgarten in Steyerberg. There they had been able to implement the ideas of permaculture and work on new forms of living together.

❖ I only know whether an idea is visionary or utopian after I have tried to put it into practice. I felt the same way about the money issue. After the long years of analysis – after waiting and hoping that the monetary system would be modified from above through the insights of 'decision-makers' working in the central bank or in politics – yet seeing that nothing significant had actually changed, the time had come to find out whether it was really possible at all, or if I should finally abandon it. It was clear to me that this would be the 'practical phase' of my twenty years of work on money. But how? Where? And with whom? At the time, I didn't know."

"That's the Vision!"

In addition to her numerous lectures and workshops, following her time working for the International Building Exhibition (IBA), Margrit taught at the Gesamthochschule (University) Kassel in 1985 and 1986, as a visiting professor for urban ecology at the Department of Landscape Planning and Urban Development. From 1991 to 2002 she worked as a professor of Building Technology and Resource Saving Building at the Department of Architecture at the University of Hanover, particularly on ecological issues. She never doubted the relevance of her work, yet it was increasingly clear to her that the natural foundations of all life were threatened and being destroyed by the flawed monetary system. Declan felt the same way.

- We both believe that a truly free and social market economy and the continuation of the current monetary system are mutually exclusive. We see how this present monetary system forces us to act more and more harshly. The system is suffocating life on this planet. "Freedom" and "Social issues" are gone. Day by day we lose a bit more of our quality of life. We must alter the course and get it back."

A Shift in the Focus of her Work

Following her memorable meeting with Helmut Creutz – with whom she then frequently corresponded and spoke with by telephone – she began to intensively study the facets new to her understanding, regarding issues in the monetary system. She presented her insights in a first essay, entitled "Women bear the greatest burdens: war, the monetary system and land law." It was published several times meeting with positive and widespread acclaim. From that point on, Margrit included the topic of money in nearly all her lectures.

❖ I now devoted 15 minutes of my ecology lectures to the money topic. The message to my audiences was: 'What I have shown you so far is promising and feasible. but it can't be realized in a big way, because... that's just the way it is with money'. And more and more often listeners would come up to me afterwards and say: 'Your lecture was very exciting, but what you said at the end about money, where can one read about this?' Unfortunately, as I understood it, there was no one else talking about it at the time. I was constantly fighting myself against my own involvement in the matter. Every time I had to give a negative response to such questions, I would argue with myself, 'No, I'm not getting involved in this subject. After all, I'm not an economist and the focus of my work is completely different.' So, I left it at that. I gave my urban ecology and permaculture lectures and spoke a bit about money at the end."

Through her encounters with Bill Mollison in 1981 and Helmut Creutz in 1982, Margrit had come to know the causes behind problems that had occupied her for many years. Well-established human modes of living, developed over long periods of time, pose an ever-increasing threat to the natural environment because of an inherent systemic compulsion for infinite growth that is incompatible with the natural order. Through Bill Mollison, the ecological dimension of the problem – and through Helmut Creutz, the economic dimension – had become completely clear to her. She had also understood which systemic flaw in the monetary system was responsible for the entire dilemma: interest and compound interest. Notably, it was Margrit's initial skepticism – that the answer could be so simple – that inspired her headlong dive into what from that moment on became her lifelong work. Was it truly the case that an entitlement to the creation of money, without concomitant physical productivity – which is the premise underlying any claim for interest – produces such serious consequences that in economic terms it actually suppresses any potential for ecological and socially meaningful modes of living?

All we have for our life on this earth is what this earth gives to us. This is a very simple but true statement. For we must recognize, in light of this circumstance, that what is available must also be enough. For example, we can consume non-renewable resources only once, and we are also dependent on specific conditions for the growth of food in our fields, insofar as fertile soil produces better harvests. Nevertheless, we've established behaviours that don't respect these natural conditions and limits. These behaviors have developed over time and they are expressed in the way we treat the earth as our habitat.

It must be seen, In the context of a basic understanding of our role as humans on this earth, that we've managed to gradually separate our concept of ourselves from nature. We now experience ourselves as human beings in a natural world that merely surrounds us. In this worldview, Nature has become the opponent, and has been devalued, relative to the human being. We know that this is a mistake that leads to fatal consequences, but in our experience of the world and in our convictions, we are so tightly bound to the premises of the prevailing economy that we quickly and willingly ignore this fact. And it's the same flaw in the monetary system that Margrit recognized in 1982 that is precisely the cause.

Whenever anyone makes a purchase, i.e. buys something edible, clothes or you name it, the goods are traded at a place that is at the end of a debt chain. The business in which one finds oneself may have been established with credit, the supplier may have leased his vehicle, the machinery in the producing factories may have been purchased with debt financing, etc. All these credit funds, which were used in the chain of production, delivery and sale, give rise to a demand for interest, which is calculated into the price of the goods by all creditors. At the end of this chain, a price is charged which now includes the "cost of money" (all interest) that has ever been accrued. The last price to be paid is therefore not only the real costs of the goods, but also the interest claims of the banks. This calculated share of interest in the price of all consumer goods in Germany is around 30 percent. This means that all consumers have to use a good third of their money to pay interest on loans, even if they themselves carry no personal debts.

In this way, the prevailing monetary and economic system forces the creation of added value that is counted exclusively in monetary units. The resulting pressure for growth is inherent in the system and ultimately forces the demand for steady, unlimited growth. This absurdity eventually causes breakdowns, because infinite growth cannot exist in a finite world. Our economy would therefore have collapsed completely long ago, had not the steep development of the exponential curve – which can be used to map the increase in the speed of our path into the abyss – been partially mitigated, again and again, by the collapse of individuals, groups of people, small or large companies or states. But what is also happening at the same time is a tremendous shifting process in the possession of money and assets from the hands of many to that of a few ultra-rich. The gap between rich and poor continues to widen, without any direct human intervention, simply because the system works the way it does.

This fact made Margrit sad and at times angry. From that point on, she dedicated all her power to do what she could to help change the system! She didn't stop at criticism, rather suggesting practical means through which this could be achieved. Once writing to a politician, she explained in concise terms how what she called "regional money", used as a complementary currency in tandem with regular currency, could play a part in the solution.

- You could easily explain this to your citizens: an average household in Germany today spends a considerable part of its annual income on interest, as it is calculated into retail prices. Some of this interest is an unavoidable cost (real bank costs, risk premiums and so on). But some could be eliminated if each household in your region covered some of its needs locally, paying for them with an interest-free local currency. For this to work, the producers of regional goods would have to pass on the savings they achieve – through interest-free loans in regional money – to their customers, but this would go a long way, wouldn't it?"

Her first book on the subject, published in August 1987, was translated into many languages and enjoyed wide circulation. As a result, Margrit was frequently invited to speak at lectures and workshops where she addressed the topic of money. At the same time, the issues of ecology became ever more important to her.

❖ The lecture, which I developed then out of Helmut Creutz's line of thought and which I have since given a hundred times, has remained, in essence, unchanged in all the ensuing years. Occasionally, people attending Helmut Creutz's lectures would say to him afterwards 'Oh, you also use Margrit Kennedy's graphs!' Although his name is on each one of these graphs, it must have been hard for him now and then. But he knew that it was not my intention to adorn myself with his plumes, and I often try to make it clear at the beginning of my lectures by explicitly thanking him, as the pioneer of this field. And I am glad that these stories have not undermined our good rapport over the years."

In 1988 Margrit was invited to give a lecture at a large conference in Bad Homburg. A local bookstore had set up a book table there, where an editor from the publishing house Goldmann was also present. The idea was conceived that Margrit's book should be re-released in a revised and expanded version. This time rather than self-published, it would be published by a large, renowned publishing house.

❖ I worked on it again for three months – significantly longer than it took for the original – to turn the 'pamphlet', as the editor jokingly called it, into a real book. I simply gave the appropriate answers to all the questions that the first edition always raised, and the book was twice as long. Still, a real book in the sense of a real publisher."

In Conflict with the System

As Margrit became increasingly involved with the monetary system and its possible alternatives and amendments, she acquired a deep understanding of the underlying tensions inherent in it. She realized with increasing certainty that the main problem interest rates pose is the assumption of infinite growth in a finite world. But there can be no such thing. Ultimately, the reality is altogether different: even in the context of a limited supply of money, it's simply a matter of redistribution, not infinite growth. The gains of one in the pursuit of money are therefore always the losses of the other. Likewise, with regard to the natural resources of the earth, there can be no infinite growth, only reckless redistribution and exploitation, which impoverishes one party and enriches another.

This principle works for a while, but then, like a pyramid scheme, necessitates partial collapses (of an individual, a group of people, a region ......) in order to continue to exist at all. At the same time, this enormous redistribution and exploitation mechanism is kept going by the system, which at some point can neither be stopped nor really controlled and mastered. Ultimately, Margrit came to realize that it has already permeated the whole of life, and no sphere has been spared its madness.

Margrit noticed how the gross financial assets of private households in Germany continues to be almost five times GDP and more than six times the debt level of the public sector. This is colossal and at the same time puzzling, as the question remains: to whom primarily are these huge amounts of money to be assigned as assets? And since the balance sheet always has two sides: to whom should the debt, corresponding to the creation of money by the banks, be assigned? By German standards alone, the answer to these questions is terrifying!

While the bottom half of private households have no significant net assets, 60 percent of total assets are concentrated in the hands of the upper 10 percent, whose wealth has steadily increased. The obvious conclusion is that the gap between rich and poor is also widening in Germany, especially as the interest on assets in turn accrues interest. And this compound interest effect leads to an exponential increase in redistribution. In fact, this means that more and more is swiftly taken out of the hands of a large section of the population and becomes the private assets of a minority. This redistribution takes place very subtly, relatively quietly and is driven by the sheer power of the money and financial system. The cost of interest, as calculated into the price of all consumer goods in Germany, is close to 30 percent. This means that one third of the money that people spend serves to pay interest rate demands that have been added into the price of goods. If one takes this into consideration, it's clear that from the point of view of the individual as well as that of the economic community, debt is always paid for, regardless of whether the individual is directly responsible for the debt or not. And both sides of the balance sheet, debts as well as assets, are growing exponentially greater and faster, at breakneck speed, up to a final, inevitable collapse. Margrit once wrote to a friend about this, also with regard to her experiences with the family business.

❖ You know, dear Gisela, it is precisely this growth principle – which has now become autonomous – that is the central dilemma of our economy. Without anyone else being able to say why, sales must increase. Stagnating turnover is a sign of weakness. If everyone acts in this way, how can it lead to success in the long run? I've seen how risks grow with an increase in size – not necessarily profit. It's a typical dilemma for medium-sized companies, in the context of the current economic situation, And I've also seen how political changes naturally influence decisions within a company. Often, this caused problems for my father. Later, during my studies, I always had trouble with discussions, which were fierce in the sixties, on the topic of 'which is better: communism or capitalism?' A lot of people who then argued belligerently for workers' rights were basically noble communists. I found it unfair how such discussions condemned my father, as the typical, evil capitalist. When I thought of the risks he took, I just couldn't join the anti-capitalist chorus. I knew the differences in responsibility, risk-taking and commitment that existed in my father's business, and therefore I could not argue for 'equal pay for all'. On the one hand, I learned about the dark side of capitalism, the harshness associated with it and the increasing polarisation between rich and poor, and on the other hand I felt it was wrong to condemn the concept of private property in general. I felt it was essential that each and every one should be able to achieve something for themselves. It was then that I began to think about how to overcome this conflict between communism and capitalism – a third option. Today I see this third path as a way of life that I try to promote through two concepts, namely permaculture as a holistic ecological concept and regional currencies as a social counterbalance to the global monetary systems. Everything we need to live – the basic supply of food, energy and land – could be organized most sensibly on a local basis. The world market can then produce that which is required beyond this. My most fervent wish has always been that everyone should have the capability to develop themselves through the greatest possible personal freedom and creativity. In this respect, I can see today that the 'entrepreneurial training' during my childhood had a decisive influence on my approach to money."

Regional Money

While money, freed from avarice and greed, can be a practical means of facilitating exchange, interest and compound interest imbue it with destructive properties inimical to life. The tool has long since become a weapon. A system whose impact on the immediate environment "as a given" may only be tolerated for a certain remaining time, as societal awareness of these issues on the whole is increasing on a massive scale. Many people ignore the fact that ever greater numbers of people are becoming impoverished in Germany, that hunger, misery and wars are spreading more rapidly in the world, responding with an apathetic "that is just the way it is, I cannot change it". But there comes a point when such suffering and contempt for human beings can no longer be simply ignored.

Through their bans on interest, which lasted for many centuries, the world's so-called great religions touched a nerve; whether we like it or not. We too are all now being sucked into a course of events – caught up in nothing less than the battle for the very survival of nature and mankind. It is high time to counter this ruthless and coercive system, central to money and all our dealings with it.

The necessity to recognise existing conditions – and to change them – had already been proposed by a number of visionary thinkers at the start of the 20th century. Among them was the merchant Silvio Gesell, whose ideas of what he called "free enterprise" were very close to Margrit's heart. Gesell countered growth-driven interest rates with a "circulation safeguard", which, as a negative interest rate on hoarded money, was intended to accelerate its circulation.

While Helmut Creutz assumed that the implementation of free economic ideas would only be possible through widespread political reforms, Margrit believed that the best way to achieve this was through many small and medium-sized systems that complemented the larger monetary system. She agreed with Bernard Lietaer, with whom she'd been in close contact since the early 1990s. From Lietaer, she had adopted the idea of "complementary currencies", which, as a supplement to the otherwise common standard currencies, are created and circulated by free, non-governmental initiative groups. Consistently with her bottom-up approach, Margrit eventually coined the terms "regional money" or "regional currency" to refer to complementary currencies, using them frequently from then on and thereby establishing them in the relevant context.

❖ Regional currencies offer very attractive benefits for counties and represent a windfall for regional development. It took me a few years to really understand this myself. Although I knew that barter networks were too small to make a noticeable difference in the way one handles the money in one's own wallet. They have done valuable pioneering work by making the idea tangible that you can create your own money. They were necessary as a first step. But they cannot cover more than one to two percent of the average necessities of life. And that's too small a sum to feel that this type of economic activity actually brings economic benefits. The European Central Bank, on the other hand, is probably too big for effective monetary reforms. For a long time, this seemed to me to be the only way, and it's not a bad idea.

But it simply takes too long. So, what's left? The middle level. The region. That's how I came up with the idea of regional currencies in the first place. Regional money isn't just about economics. I believe that it is a great advantage for the inhabitants of a region to have an instrument at their disposal that enables everyone to benefit their living environment. People no longer need feel so helplessly at the mercy of global developments, over which they have no influence. This strengthens their identity with their local community, their district, and the identification of each and every individual with the region."

The idea of regional currencies and the effects they have on the economy was also inspired by Margrits memories of her own childhood, during which she was able to experience the still largely functioning local economy. Now it became clear how she could combine her experience as an architect with her ideas for a different monetary system by presenting the advantages of regional currencies in concrete terms.

❖ When I was a child, each village had its own specialty shop. Whether bread or cheese, woodcarving and fabrics or pottery, everything was different from the neighbouring village, which was only a few kilometers away. Today, we have uniform city centres and pedestrian zones all over the country, and in the villages we always see the same three or four brands and retail chains. I see this homogenization as a loss of the wealth and diversity that once characterised our country. It will not be possible to restore it completely. But I am sure that the regional currencies can help to stop this tendency towards desolation.

- A regional currency has advantages for all the inhabitants of a region in all walks of life. For example, for the citizens as consumers: If we assume that about thirty percent of the necessities of life can be obtained in the region. If a regional currency of this magnitude allows us to break away from the interest-dominated Euro system, then real savings and new value chains are possible. Regional money increases the liquidity of companies through interest-free or reduced-interest loans and thus the opportunity to invest. And it facilitates a closer relationship with customers. As initial experience has shown, increased sales in the region are a given, after a certain start-up period.

- My strongest hope is that regional money will help to guarantee the basic provision of people's needs in the region and that the regions regain enough self-sufficiency to make it easier to survive, in times of need. Food and water supply, energy supply, sewage and waste disposal. In other words, the basic things we need for a reasonably good life, would have to be secured in the region. Of course, it is also possible to trade with neighbouring regions, but the basic services would not, in any case, have to be sold to American or other private investors, as we are now increasingly seeing.

- Yes, I hope that with the help of the regional currencies we will manage to keep, improve and stabilize these fundamental things in the region – and to do so as ecologically as possible and independently of large corporations and world market prices.

- That's the vision!"

With brother Reinhard and father Kurt Hübner, 1983

In Norway, 1985

Daughter Antja, 1987

Kennedy house in Steyerberg, 1985

and 1988

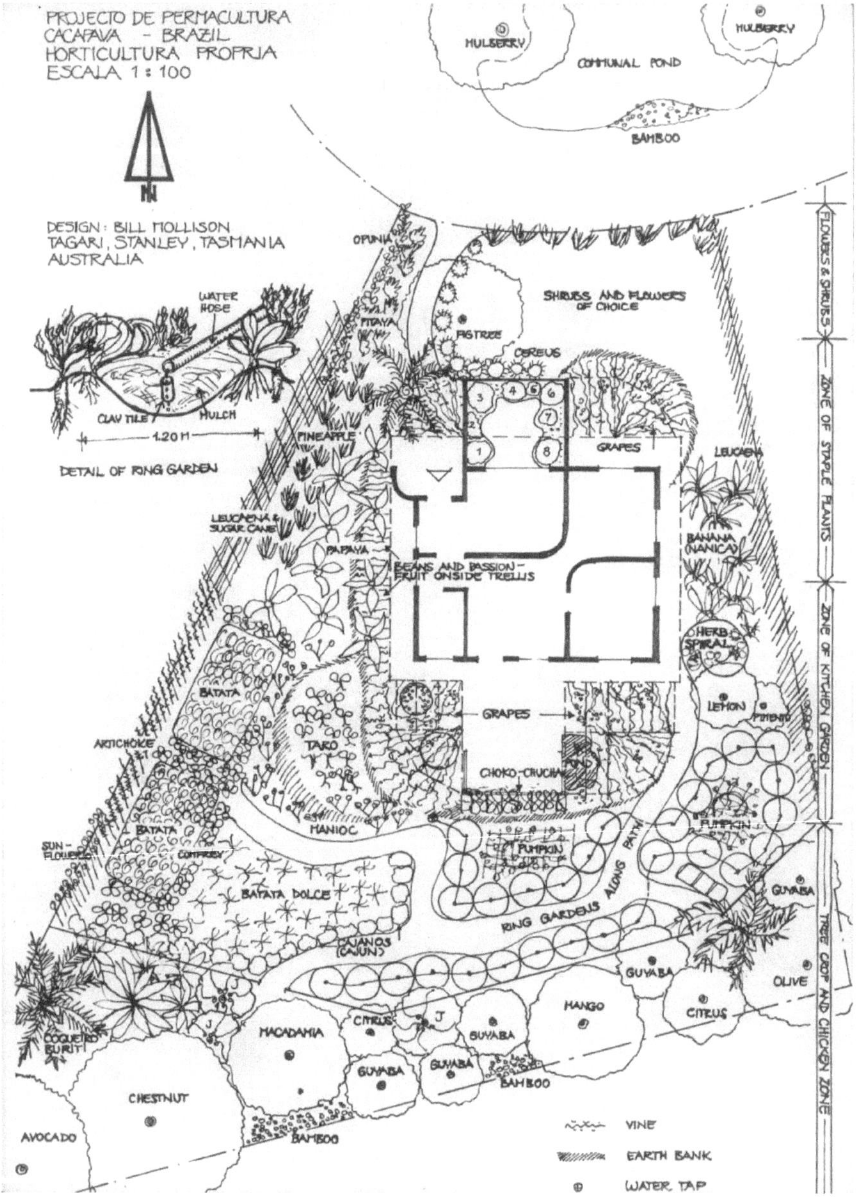

Design with Bill Mollison in Brasil, 1981

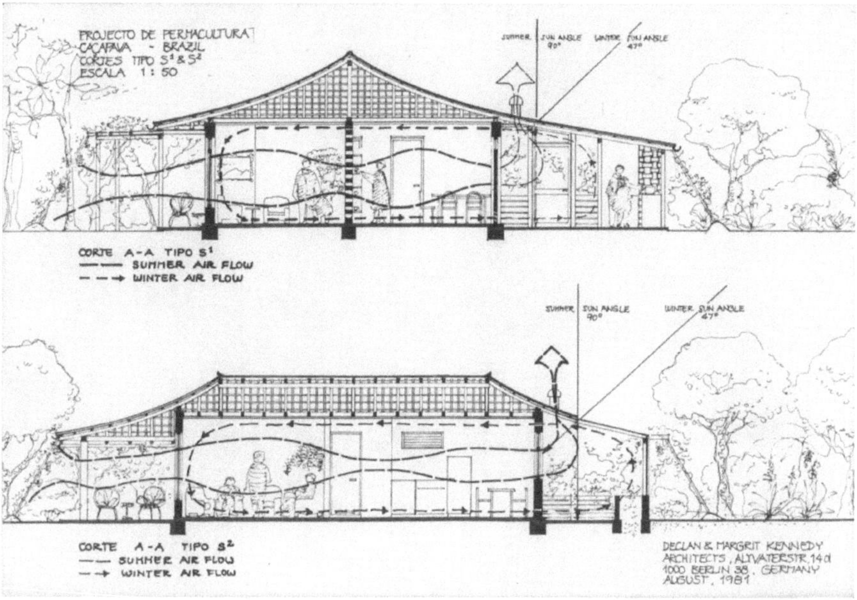

Section through worker's house in Caçapava, Brasil
design by Margrit Kennedy, 1981
implementation by Declan Kennedy, 1982

A Global Commitment to Complementary Currencies (2001 – 2013)

Many people inspired Margrit to develop her own ideas and work. One such person was the American woman Genevieve Vaughan, also born on November 21, 1939, who was intensely engaged with the gift economy, but from a female perspective. Margrit had invited her for a workshop on this topic at Lebensgarten. As Margrit's yearning grew to implement practically her ideas on regional money, she and Declan set off on a trip around the world lasting several months, in the fall of 2001. The Kennedys had been invited to give lectures by the "Wise Women of the World". First, they travelled to London, then to Halifax, Canada and Cali, Columbia. An increasing number of requests resulted in a travel route that included a diverse range of countries and cities. In total, the Kennedys gave 80 lectures, over the four and a half months of their world trip.

World Tour

They travelled to Colombia at the invitation of the lawyer and politician Angela Cuevas de Dolmetsch, Ph.D., who had met Margrit three months earlier at a

"Wise Women of the World" conference in Norway. In Cali, Margrit shared her ideas through a number of presentations, at times attended by politicians and municipal administration staff; and developed a concept for circulating safeguarded regional money. So, the transition to practical implementation was indeed successful, especially because there were already original self-help projects taking place in Cali.

❖ In Colombia we had an interesting encounter with a man, the husband of our friend Angela de Cuevas de Dolmetsch. He was English by birth and worked as a flautist and artistic director of the Symphony Orchestra in Cali. His father, grandfather and great-grandfather were also flute makers in London and he owned flutes of all sizes and woods. Aside from giving concerts in the beautiful opera of Cali, he worked with a circus, where only street children were admitted. To bring classical music to these girls and boys, he thought up something wonderful: he had the street kids and youngsters from the circus school perform at the opera house. While they appeared on stage as jugglers and tightrope walkers, the symphony orchestra played accompanying classical pieces. Once our friend from the orchestra climbed onto the stage himself and played as a flutist with his flutes, from the smallest to the largest. In the late mornings, the symphony orchestra and the street children played for the school children without charging admission, and in the evenings the adults came to the concert and paid. I was deeply impressed that the people in these countries, despite their poverty, take music and theatre, and culture in general, so seriously. But our friend's argument was very practical. 'If we don't get the children together with classical music at an early age, one day we won't have an audience anymore', he said."

From Cali they travelled via Los Angeles to New Zealand. The Kennedys had sent only two e-mails to their friends there, offering to give talks on money reform and eco-villages, but received twenty-eight invitations in just two weeks. So, they spent two months there. Margrit also talked about the regional currency solution which she had invented in Cali, using rough calculations for the various New Zealand regions. And with each presentation, the proposals became more concrete and they were met with increasing enthusiasm.

❖ Together with my friend Deirdre Kent in Wellington, I finally tried to work out the first version of a new, co-written book. Declan had flown a few days earlier to Byron Bay, Australia, where he was invited to lecture."

At a meeting with the US-American Leonard Orr, the inventor of the rebirthing process and a proponent of new money models, which were primarily intended to make paying taxes superfluous, Margrit had learned about the "Save Australia Buyers Club", which had developed a voucher system with which Australian companies were to be bought back from foreign investors. Declan arranged a meeting with Robert Walsch, the inventor of the system. Margrit wanted to meet him as soon as possible after her arrival in Brisbane, Queensland in northwest Australia, to find out more. The concept of a voucher system seemed to her to be a good way of implementing her idea of a regional currency.

The "Save Australia Buyers Club" had found out that eighty percent of Australian companies now belonged to foreigners, most of whom transferred their profits to the nearby tax haven of Cooks Island, while only six percent paid tax in Australia. The aim was to counteract this practice, which had been devastating for the regional economy. Robert Walsch explained to Margrit that the "Save Australia Buyers Club" had some time ago started to issue vouchers worth $110 at a price of $100, which could be used to make purchases from local companies.

- The project was a complete success: In Gympie, an otherwise rather conservative city north of Brisbane where the model worked, the companies exchanged seventy percent of the vouchers back into dollars in the first year, and only seven percent in the third year. The voucher thus became a substitute for cash. And the only supermarket that did not accept the vouchers went bankrupt during the first three years. But in the end, the whole thing failed. I got this information two years later from Deirdre Kent, who visited Gympie to see how the whole thing was progressing. At some point, the banking regulators came and found that the organization was acting like a bank, taking deposits and giving loans – and they needed a banking license to do that, but they didn't have a banking license. Declan immediately understood that the original approach of this model, which was to issue vouchers and thus introduce a regional currency, could be the practical solution we were looking for. With Declan, I was sitting on the shore of a lake in the evening and we were discussing how the voucher system could be turned into a functioning, self-financing regional currency that could be transferred to Germany. In other words, how the business idea could be turned into a charitable cause that would belong to the people in the region and could be democratically controlled."

The time was now ripe to implement her regional money idea. After the time in Australia was over, they went on to India, where Margrit presented the idea with the vouchers as a regional currency in the eco-city of Auroville. In this "universal city" founded on February 28, 1968 and based on the social theory of Sri Aurobindo, the idea of a regional currency was well received. It was possible to directly link the ideals for living together in Auroville to a regional currency that creates and maintains community. And although the functioning of a regional currency is independent of any spiritual orientation, the intellectual roots of Auroville nevertheless provide a suitable framework.

Concentrated in a few sentences, the city's charter outlines: "Auroville belongs to nobody in particular. Auroville belongs to humanity as a whole. But, to live in Auroville, one must be a willing servitor of the Divine Consciousness. Auroville will be the place of an unending education, of constant progress, and a youth that never ages. Auroville wants to be the bridge between the past and the future. Taking advantage of all discoveries from without and from within, Auroville will boldly spring towards future realisations. Auroville will be a site of material and spiritual research for a living embodiment of an actual human unity."

After her return to Germany, the idea of a regional currency based on vouchers continued to fascinate Margrit. Soon a regional currency: the *Chiemgauer*, would be established and is still a success today.

The Money Expert

Margrit's voluntary early retirement as a professor in 2002 was a defining moment in her life. While giving up teaching at the university, she still continued to work at times as an architect, through projects with other architectural offices. However, she now saw the monetary issue as the focus of her, work especially as initiative groups were gradually forming to deal with the practical implementation of regional currencies. Margrit's expertise played an important role in this, but it was also valued by experts around the world. And sometimes her ideas made their way through surprising channels:

- ❖ When I was invited to Delitzsch in 2002, where the first bank in Germany wanted to introduce a regional complementary currency, the savings bank director picked me up from the train station with his friend. My first money book was in the front of the car. 'Do you know who I got it from?' asked the friend. 'No', I said, 'how should I know?' 'Your mother gave it to me,' he said, when he'd met her at a conference in Switzerland. When she heard he was a banker, she gave him my book and said: 'Perhaps you can do more with it than I can.' He left it unnoticed for a long time, and when he finally read it, it completely changed his picture of what he was doing professionally. And eventually he left the banking business, not without first infecting his friend, the savings bank director in Delitzsch. The latter was then involved in his bank being the first to lay the foundations for the introduction of a regional currency. So, my mother was ultimately one of the initiators of the first bank in the regional money movement. I could feel how happy my mother was 'up there' at that moment as I stood at the Delitzscher railway station, completely surprised by this story."

In the same year, Margrit was invited to a meeting with regional managers in Hesselberg by the friendly business consultant Peter Bauer. At that time, Bauer advised local authorities and districts participating in the EU's LEADER Plus programme, for the promotion of disadvantaged regions. He learned time and again that the biggest problem was that public budgets lacked the money to implement the ideas developed in forward-looking conferences. Yes, Margrit knew this problem well, because during her time in Berlin she was repeatedly told that ecologically sensible projects would not pay off.

That was one of the reasons why she had started to look at possible alternatives to the prevailing monetary system that could free ecologically sensible projects from the existing economic constraints.

❖ That is why I presented my findings and suggestions to three regional managers and Bernd Reuther, a pastor who headed the Hesselberg Lutheran Adult Education Center. They were enthusiastic and became immediately involved. That was my entry into the reality of the regions. Since then I have been supporting these cognitive processes wherever I can. And now at least five LEADER-Plus regions, i.e. those participating in this EU funding programme for regions in the German-speaking world, have incorporated the issue of money into their development activities."

The name LEADER stands for "*Liaison Entre Actions de Développement de l'Économie Rurale*" (link between actions for the development of the rural economy) and is a programme that supports projects in rural areas. Its main aim is to establish local partnerships between the public, private, social and economic sectors and to network with neighbouring regions.

After the successful completion of two previous funding phases, the European Union introduced the LEADER-Plus Programme, which increased the number of LEADER-Plus regions in Germany to 148.

Through contact with this program, Margrit was also invited to a lecture in the Upper Palatinate, attended by forty regional managers who, it soon turned out, were a critical audience. It was apparent that most of those present were initially closed-minded about the innovative character and the possible positive effects of regional currencies, which is why Margrit was literally blanketed with counter arguments.

❖ At some point, the district administrator who had invited me had had enough of the objections, stood up and said: 'You know, gentlemen, this is all well and good what you are presenting here. But at the moment it seems to me that the only person in this room who represents a new paradigm and can contribute practical ideas is Mrs. Kennedy!' A female mayor from Eastern Bavaria told me afterwards: 'I liked your regional approach anyway, but these social and cultural aspects were not so clear to me. Now I understand the scope of this issue!'"

Margrit already knew the district administrator before this event. She respected him because he had campaigned for ecological solutions for a variety of projects. At his initiative, Germany's largest solar system, at that time, was installed in Neumarkt. The fact that the district council was headed by the CSU (the conservative party of Bavaria) in no way diminished Margrit's esteem, because it was clear to her that it was necessary for ecological initiatives to be developed across party lines in order to be really successful.

***

It was at one of the 13 "Money Conferences" in Lebensgarten, in 2002, that Margrit had her first memorable encounter with Christian Gelleri, a teacher from the Waldorf school in Prien who had been working for some time on alternative ideas to the monetary system. Upon meeting him she exclaimed with astonishment, "You're so young!" Their professional contact was thus established and grew deeper in succeeding years. Gelleri, who was already familiar with Silvio Gesell's ideas from his family home, had read Margrit's book "Interest and Inflation Free Money" at the beginning of the 1990s, and had then started to work on ideas for its concrete implementation. He was inspired by the initiative for direct democracy launched by the artist Johannes Stüttgen, who Margrit also knew and respected. The moment had obviously come when the implementation of a regional currency could begin. Bernard Lietaer acted as an advisor on conceptual issues, while Margrit advised on practical ones.

More than eighty people from twenty-two countries had come to the money meeting. Christian Gelleri wasn't the only one encouraged to implement the voucher idea; another fifteen initiators from various regions also signaled that they too were ready to launch regional currencies. Margrit was thrilled, because it seemed that the moment had clearly come, and the subject that had occupied her thoughts for so long could now become a tangible reality. In fact, nothing could forestall the advent of this new movement, out of which a growing number of regional currency projects were to emerge in the years to come. As a result, the scope of Margrit's consulting and lecturing activities steadily expanded.

- My hope is that one day the regional banks will take over the management, just as the large construction companies, who at first thought it ridiculous, are now also offering ecological products. However, it should remain the way it is now being started by the *Regiogeld* (Regio cash) initiators, namely with a high level of public benefit, transparency and democratic control. Of course, the banks would be paid for their work: e.g. the salaries of their employees, the upkeep of the premises. But beyond that, it is not individuals who will benefit excessively (as is the case in today's monetary system for the owners of money), but the region that gives itself this money".

Argentina: "Credito" and "Mar y Sierra"

In her consulting work, Margrit was able to draw on a wealth of experience that she had gathered over time all over the world. This included her encounter with the "Credito", the Argentinean complementary currency that had ensured the survival of millions of people for many years during the great economic crisis there from 1998 to 2002.

Argentina went through a severe recession in 1998 and 1999 and the financial system collapsed in 2001. The poverty rate in the country rose to 57 percent and the national debt in foreign currency to 92 percent. This was an extraordinarily bad situation for Argentina, which had been one of the richest countries in the world in the first half of the 20th century. A complementary currency, the Credito, provided very effective support for the population's own efforts in self-sufficiency. Margrit had met two of its founders in Hanover when she had just left the university. Ruben and Carlos had read the Spanish translation of Margrit's book and were now eager to meet her personally on their trip to Europe.

First, however, a language difficulty had to be overcome: the two Argentineans spoke little English and Margrit only a little Spanish. Somehow, they managed and Margrit listened spellbound to what the two had to tell her now.

❖ I heard that women in particular were the important multipliers of this system. Then Carlos pulled out a completely worn out copy of the Spanish translation of my book: 'We found this after we introduced the Credito. It is the theory behind what we have done in practice. Now there are quite a few difficulties and we need you. Please help us to cope with it.' Of course, I was happy to be needed in this context. I had already heard that complementary currencies had become extremely important after the collapse of the entire monetary system in Argentina. But I didn't know exactly how and to what extent. So, what better thing could happen to me than to be invited to a country where my theory was 'lived'? It was very exciting! The one hour we had set aside for the meeting became two. Then we went out for dinner, and had another final meeting a few days later, in Steyerberg. Carlos and Ruben promised to bring a translator: 'We met a Chilean on the train. He's an interpreter, and when we told him about our request, he immediately agreed to translate for us'. As it later turned out, it was Alvaros, a good friend of my Chilean colleague Prof. Eduardo Vargas, who (until his sudden death of a few years previously) had been one of my closest friends at the university".

A few days later Carlos, Ruben and Alvaros came to Steyerberg as agreed to talk to Margrit and Declan about the Credito and the situation in Argentina. The group gathered in the Kennedys' conservatory and worked for five hours. Flipcharts were explained and diagrams were drawn.

❖ I wanted to understand in detail what exactly was going on there in Argentina, how the Credito worked and where the difficulties were now. Carlos and Ruben were very keen that I understand the full scope of their initiative. They were completely convinced that they could save the world and that they had done the best they could. And I believed them."

The Credito had spread quickly from a suburb of Buenos Aires. By the time the economic crisis began in 2000, 15,000 people were already participating in the system, and the number was growing after the peso suddenly lost eighty percent of its value overnight. The Credito's radius soon covered the whole of Argentina. Now it was practically impossible for the organizers to trace and check who, what and where was happening with the Credito.

Eventually the first forgeries came into circulation. Carlos and Ruben explained that the government itself might have been behind this, in order to inflate and bring down the Credito. The reason, they suspected, was envy over its success and anger over lost tax revenues. In order to make counterfeiting less likely in the future, Margrit now put Carlos and Ruben in touch with a printing company that specialized in the production of safe-guarded banknotes. She responded overall with great sympathy to the concerns of her two visitors, who she experienced as fundamentally honest people with an important concern. And she was particularly impressed by the history of the Credito's origins:

- The way the Credito came into being is wonderful: Carlos had a neighbor who planted a pumpkin. This pumpkin grew and grew and grew, over the garage on Carlos' property. And there the plant still produced the most wonderful pumpkins. He asked his neighbour if he could harvest the pumpkins on his side of the garage and offered her apples from his trees, which bore too much fruit for his needs. Thus, they exchanged what each of them had in abundance. So, the real question was: What do we do with our abundance? In other words, 'share the surplus', a basic principle of permaculture.

- When the two of them talked about it with other neighbours, who also had too much of one thing in their gardens and too little of another, more and more people from the area began to take part in the lively bartering. It was extremely practical, and everyone was able to save their scarce funds. Clothes and services were also gradually included. In order to organize things a bit better, the participants decided to introduce vouchers, which were issued by a central office and worked like money. And because they were not recognized as money by the state, they did not incur any tax liabilities."

At the end of the meeting Margrit and Declan agreed to travel to Argentina in the autumn. And in order to facilitate future understanding, they planned to attend a four-week Spanish course there.

- ❖ When we landed in Buenos Aires, it wasn't only Carlos and Ruben waiting at the airport, but also Horatio – the third initiator of the Credito – and three other members of their group. Then there was Carlos Louge, a lawyer who had found me and contacted me through the Internet, and immediately. When I wrote him that I was coming to Argentina he offered his help in organizing our stay. The moment he showed up, the atmosphere became tense and the group around Carlos, Ruben and Horatio became rather quiet. It was only later that we understood: they felt they had to leave the field to the middle-class lawyer, because they themselves felt that they belonged to the lower class. The next day we drove with the whole entourage including Carlos Louge to Silvia and Gustav Balado. Silvia is a woman who knows Declan from the Global Ecovillage Network (GEN) scene. She had started a permaculture project on the grounds of an ecovillage that was only a quarter finished at that time. In a still very primitive seminar house, she had cooked spaghetti for us. And there were certainly twenty of us. Here at the long table we had a real discussion. Many questions back and forth, a very open discussion on a high level. But we had the vague feeling that something was not being said and remained under the surface; a suspicion that would later be reinforced and finally confirmed. In any case, we got the impression that the Credito initiators group wanted to capture as much information of mine as possible on film. I was there to learn Spanish, not to give lectures, but of course I explained what I was interested in and then I asked a lot of questions, which they answered quite honestly. And still, somehow, the situation was never fully transparent for me."

The impression that something hidden, not good, was going on in the conversations was soon confirmed, when Heloisa Primavera, a professor of economics in Buenos Aires, who had been in contact with Margrit before she left for Argentina, came to visit and urgently warned the Kennedys. She reported that the Credito initiators had distributed the vouchers to friends in an uncontrolled manner and were operating chaotically in organisational matters, without concrete strategy. Margrit and Declan, who had come to have a look around and to learn Spanish, had been announced as experts from Germany who had come to make sure that the Credito found its way back into orderly channels. As proof, Primavera had brought the corresponding newspaper article. Apparently, Margrit and Declan were now caught up in a genuine intrigue.

But events took a more positive turn when, on Heloisa Primavera's recommendation, they came into contact with a group that operated a regional currency in Mar del Plata that was managed in an orderly and democratic manner. Without further ado, the Kennedys attended a meeting of the group called "Mar y Sierra" (sea and mountain).

- We immediately came into conversation with the people, as they crowded into the entrance area of a large school building. More and more people sat in a circle around us. Everyone was happy that we were interested in their cause. These people also thought that the Credito group was criminal. Of course, we wanted to know why. 'They throw the money at you', they said. 'As strangers, you can't even buy it from us.' Only registered members could get the vouchers, which was confirmed later: At the market the next day I asked one of the saleswomen if she would give me a whole series of this currency against dollars or pesos. She would be happy to do so, she said, but then she would risk being expelled from the group, and that was not worth it to her. On a later visit to another market, where they traded in Creditos, we were able to get as many Creditos as we wanted."

Towards the end of their stay, Margrit and Declan were invited by their Spanish teachers and their husbands to a place where they could experience the best tango. Of course, they wanted to try it themselves, so the dancing couples were invited by the Kennedys to give them some lessons the next day before their departure. No sooner said than done! The tango lessons took place in the hotel in the evening with many of the guests dancing along. In this way it came to an unforgettable beautiful farewell to Argentina.

***

The experience gained in Argentina was very valuable for further work on the spread of regional currencies. Important conditions were identified as a result of the tensions and disruptions experienced, as well as due to the successful system in Mar del Plata. This is how Margrit put it:

- Firstly: In times when everything is still going well, ensure that a regional currency is placed on an organizationally secure foundation. Second, the spread of a single system to other regions, i.e. the transition from a regional to a national complementary currency, does not make sense and involves numerous dangers. Third, the vouchers must be tamper-proof. Fourth, the system must be controlled democratically. A manageable region to which people feel they belong makes a certain control possible. A personality cult is only harmful. Amateurs and enthusiasm are not enough to create a working currency. We have already had this experience through countless barter networks. To redesign the monetary system, professional work and a qualified organization are necessary. I pointed this out right from the start. The *Regiogeld* (Regional cash) movement was founded in Germany, and it is taken seriously to a large extent in the *Regiogeldverband* (the Federation of Regional Cash Groups)."

Professional Structures: MonNetA and the Regiogeldverband

Margrit also gained a lot of experience in many other countries through her consulting work. In Eastern Europe, she noticed how desperately people struggled with the collapse of the communist system and the poverty that had set in, despite a relatively good supply situation. And in Russia, she noticed how, in an early capitalist manner, mafia-like organizations quickly made use of new technologies to "squeeze everything out" of the country. She experienced the people who were doing an honest job to earn a living as losers in a macabre game. Of course, complementary currencies would be a good solution to strengthen regional economic cycles, on the basis of real distributive justice.

In order to be able to meet the increasing tasks in a professional framework, Margrit founded MonNetA (Money Network Alliance) in 2003 as an Ltd. (limited liability) charitable company parallel to the Lebensgarten community. Under this umbrella, she began to bring people together and network with those who had expertise in the field of complementary currencies. This made it possible to share the information more widely and spread responsibilities among many actors. In January of the same year she was invited to give the opening speech at the official launch of the *Chiemgauer* regional currency in Prien.

❖ This was an absolutely fascinating experience for me. What commitment, what fire was there! But there were also ideal conditions with Christian Gelleri, the calm and competent teacher, and these seven pretty female students. Together they had developed this experiment from their economics lessons at the Waldorf School. Christian always let the girls run with it, staying in the background himself, until he was needed. Really impressive how he did it! That's also his great talent: he can inspire the people around him. Of course, that's teamwork. But it needs someone who has the confidence that the idea is feasible. As it later turned out, the *Chiemgauer* was the second model for a regional currency. The first model in Germany, which was called regional currency. The *Roland* had already been developed in Bremen, a city very close to us. There, too, an anthroposophical group had created a currency that was intended, above all, to support organic farming. And when the time is ripe, synchronicities simply happen!"

Margrit's lectures on regional currencies at various locations always sparked enthusiasm among people. The ensuing lively discussions often lasted many hours into the night. At an event in Schleswig, which was attended by 120 people, it was finally decided at midnight to end the discussion. Otherwise, the talks might have continued until early the next morning! Margrit was never interested in merely criticizing the existing conditions, but always in pointing out alternatives and encouraging action.

- Perhaps there are some people who only use the monetary system for their own benefit. But they can only be successful because most of us have internalized this money taboo, and thus the neo-liberal growth philosophy has been able to make its unimpeded triumphal march around the world. That is why I am concerned with education and applicable models of complementary currencies that show that there are other ways of doing things, rather than finding the 'culprits'. Look at the French, Russian and Chinese revolutions. There, a few people who had become rich at the expense of others were beheaded, but the monetary system remained unchanged. And after a short time, a new elite was at the helm. After a few decades, there was a new layer of rich and super-rich and the whole horrible game started all over again. No, this time enough people have to understand what it's all about in relation to our monetary system, and this has to be taught in school if possible. Everything else is just another temporary solution."

On the subject of "social movements", Margrit was close to the ideas of Nicanor Perlas, who in his book "Shaping Globalization. Civil Society, Cultural Power and Tripartite" shows that civil society plays a key role in the cultural area of social life because it can act as a balancing force between the state and the market. And the regional currencies made it clear time and again how concrete civil society engagement can permanently change social conditions:

- A producer of sheep and goat cheese delivers to the whole of Germany, but in his own region he sells almost nothing. The *Chiemgauer* initiators ask him if he would participate in the regional currency and accept *Chiemgauer*. 'And where can I get rid of them again?' he wanted to know. 'Which farmer do you get your milk from?' the club members ask. Together they go to the farmer: 'Would you accept the regional currency from the cheese manufacturer if he paid you with it?' 'Yes', says the farmer, 'if I can use it to buy in the shop again, I will.' So, the initiators pull out a list of shops that are willing to accept *Chiemgauer* – now five hundred in and around Prien. The farmer is then prepared to sell his milk to the cheese producer for regional money. And suddenly the cheese producer is also delivering to the region. He has now hired two extra people, and business is booming."

The work for the further spreading of the idea of regional currency was made much easier by the now common computers. If a while ago Margrit had employed two people in her office in the university in Hanover and in Steyerberg for the correspondence to be dealt with, she was now able to do much more in less time alone. She quickly got used to using a computer. Even the daily exchange with Declan – Margrit worked in her office in Lebensgarten's main building, Declan in the home office – was done via e-mail so that the two could discuss current events and ideas during their lunch break.

In the same year in which MonNetA was founded, the *Regiogeldverband* was formed in September within the framework of an association with initially forty members who represented twenty-four initiatives. Now a common, professionally organised representation of common interests was possible and the founding initiatives found a helpful support and opportunity to exchange questions and experiences.

***

During this eventful period, Bernard Lietaer was also intensively involved in the development and distribution work. He also took part in the annual conferences in Steyerberg from time to time. The series of conferences, which for many years were alternately held in English and German, had begun with small groups of experts, which grew steadily. In 2000, the conference had mainly dealt with the Terra Currency, which had been conceived by Lietaer as a complementary world reference currency.

The collaboration between Margrit and Bernard Lietaer had become ever more intensive, especially since their first personal meeting in 1999. In 2003, when Lietaer lived near Steyerberg for a while, another stage of his collaboration with Margrit began. The Riemann publishing house had asked Margrit if she would like to write another book on the subject of regional money. When she told Lietaer about it, he suggested they do it together, because he had already written some articles that could be used in this context.

Moreover, in a conversation with an old friend at the Belgian Central Bank, he had just learned about his discovery of medieval regional currencies. The two of them actually got down to business, and in March 2004 the jointly written book "Regional Currencies – New Ways to Sustainable Prosperity" was published in German, giving a great boost to the regional currency movement. A few years later, it was completely revised and updated by John Rogers and published under the title "People Money" in English.

The year of the first edition's publication, Margrit took part as a speaker in Kobe, Japan, at a conference on the topic of money, and Lietaer participated via internet.

***

In November 2004, Margrit was awarded the "Sterntaler" prize of the regional money movement, which was then awarded for the first time, in a festive ceremony. In her acceptance speech, Margrit emphasized that she shared the prize with her husband Declan, to whom she was very grateful for his years of unwavering encouragement and support. In the meantime, numerous other people have also successfully committed themselves to the regional money idea with their own projects. For example, Ralf Becker, who, as a graduate economist, had dealt with the international financial markets for many years and now conducted a training course in regional currencies that he himself had designed. Thirty-six interested people had already taken part in the first course, which was held at Lebensgarten.

The Social Sculpture and Momo

As is the case in other areas of life, the *Regiogeld* movement's most significant effects often came about spontaneously through the interaction of the many people involved. This resulted in more visibility and effectiveness than might have been achieved through the sum of individual actions.

Something entirely new, something that had never been thought of before, was emerging. The artist Joseph Beuys described such processes as the workings of a "social sculpture" pointing to a spiritual dimension that under suitable conditions can be consciously tapped. Margrit was familiar with these ideas, as Joseph Beuys had also incorporated them into his *Documenta* contributions. And it was one of Beuys' master students, Johannes Stüttgen, who brought the concept to the *Regiogeld* movement.

❖ I fondly remember Johannes Stüttgen's lectures, which put our practical work into a larger framework and gave it new depth. Johannes, an artist and pupil of Joseph Beuys, had once again broadened my view with his diagram of the economic cycle and social sculpture. I find it liberating when someone reveals the spiritual dimension that lies behind the outer form. And Johannes Stüttgen was thrilled to meet people who bring what he places in the spiritual into reality. In this respect we complemented each other well. What really won me over was his picture with the wall: how we constantly try to run our heads through the wall with our terms and concepts. On the other side is the future, and we want to get there by means of violence and old ways of behaving. And yet the door in the wall opens inwards – towards us!"

Margrit's high regard for Johannes Stüttgen's works illustrates once again the importance she accorded to the artistic expression of social issues. But it was also the other way around, in so far as artists recognized the importance of Margrit's work. As an example, her book "Interest and Inflation Free Money" turned up in Michael Ende's estate – which leads to a remarkable story that Margrit first learned of during her visit to Japan. She was there as a speaker at a conference held on the occasion of the tenth anniversary of a terrible earthquake and was warmly welcomed by many participants. They already knew her from television, they said which Margrit could not make any sense of, at first, until she remembered at some point that a Japanese film team had come to Steyerberg to interview her. She hadn't heard anything more from these people after that. But she had been sent a book, though other than the recognizable graphics, she was unable to read it, as it was all in Japanese.

She later learned that this book was about Michael Ende and his "Momo" story. The Japanese assumed that the gray men, referred to in the book as the time thieves, meant they themselves. What Margrit didn't realize was that the filmmakers had made the film, which was a huge success in Japan, as if time was synonymous with money, and as if Momo was Margrit.

- As if my ideas about money, how to organize it better, could defeat the thieves who are stealing our life-energy in our unjust societies today! In the story of Momo, nearly all of my first book is wrapped up in the form of a fairy tale. That's how people in Japan understood it. So the film was such a big success that they made a book out of it as well. Inside was a summary of my money book and a photo of me. Everywhere I was invited to give talks during my lecture tour in Japan, I encountered people with this book in their hands. They wanted me to sign it. And since I didn't know the film, I could only guess from the reaction of the Japanese how much what I had written had meant to them. It was as if I had strewn a bag of seeds, and the flowers suddenly grew in a place where I had not expected it at all. It was quite an amazing discovery."

The Global Crisis

In addition to regional issues, Margrit was always keeping an eye on global developments. Debt relief for the poorest countries in the world, announced in Edinburgh in 2005, was an admission that the monetary system was not working. The interest burden was so overwhelming that these countries would never be able to free themselves from their debt loads.

The politicians of the world's economic powers had evidently reached this conclusion.

The global economic situation became increasingly acute. And to Margrit, the alarming facts were absolutely clear: there had already been a departure from the real economy to a distressing degree due to the rapidly increasing trend of speculation.

Only less than four percent of the global money supply in circulation was now being used to pay for real services in daily life. All other money had since then been used for speculation in the market for stocks, currencies and derivatives. The collapse of the ever more fragile financial market seemed not only possible, but quite probable. But let's take a closer look at what it was all about and to what disastrous consequences it finally led.

Whose world is it? Insofar as the question relates to world assets previously recorded in monetary values, 86.2 percent of these are owned by the richest ten percent of the population. This fact alone ought to make one sit up and listen. But we can analyze it even more closely, which leads to the result that 85 people own 50 percent of the world's wealth. 85! A class of super-rich individuals has emerged, notably in the last 40 years, juxtaposed to billions of super-poor individuals (the poor half of the world's population has to be content with owning only one percent of the world's wealth). In a 2005 "Citigroup Report", a term is used to describe this desired and promoted development of the world's population towards an "hourglass economy": plutonomy.

In order to spur this kind of economic development, and steadily enrich themselves, they took advantage of the fact – starting as early as the 1970s – that mere claims of assets, in other words "assets not yet existing", could also be considered part of their total assets. On a balance sheet, a claim is always a made-up number when viewed in real economic terms. Let's assume, somewhat exaggeratedly, it's a justifiable contingency (a claim merely expressing that upon payment by a debtor, a certain amount of money would actually be available as assets – not "is available").

If, for example, someone buys a house for 250,000 Euros without equity capital, for which he obtains a loan of 300,000 Euros (i.e. 120 percent) from a bank. At the same time a claim for interest arises, through this loan which the bank can sell to another bank, a fund or the like, in order to immediately benefit from the anticipated future loan repayment. And this is exactly what happens on a large scale worldwide in ever longer chains of trade and speculation.

In 1977, a certain Robert Dall, known as the "mastermind of mortgage-backed bonds", came up with an idea that made the world a completely different place in no time at all: He saw debt as a great speculative instrument and through his job as a partner at the investment bank "Salomon Brothers", bundled mortgages (mostly those on single-family homes) valued at $100 million. With this comparatively small package, a previously unknown trade in related securities was launched.

Since the acquisition of real estate as an expression of the "American way of life" was state-subsidized, the total amount of these loans increased from $55 billion in 1950 to $700 billion in 1976. With the implementation of Robert Dall's idea, this sum exploded in just four more years to a total of $1.2 trillion by 1980. The bubble kept expanding. The real estate market was now outperforming the stock market, becoming the largest capital market in the world. What this translates into is that countless people have deliberately and unscrupulously been driven to ever-increasing levels of personal debt. It corresponds with Citigroup's express business policy (Citigroup, incidentally, bought "Salomon Brothers" in 1998). Their 2005 annual report reassuringly suggested that "social unrest is no cause for concern". Just two years later, the entire bubble would burst, and millions of formerly well-off people lost everything they owned, landing on the streets in bitter poverty. The tragic irony in it all was that to save the "too-big-to-fail" banks, the government paid $1,600 billion to offset the losses. And this went straight into the pockets of the super-rich owners of the banks.

Instead of coming to our senses after this catastrophe, this very same "game" is still being played, even in Germany. This results in a fight for survival among the normal population.

***

The global economic and financial crisis, which began in 2007, prompted Margrit to step up her activities. While developing damage-control strategies for complementary currencies, she also worked to expand self-sufficiency in the permaculture park at her place of residence, the ecovillage in Steyerberg, which had now already been in existence for twenty years.

From 2005, Margrit participated in the "World Future Council", which Jakob von Uexküll, the founder of the Right Livelihood Award, established in 2004 to promote a policy of sustainability and justice as the "voice of future generations". In 2008 she met the Egyptian Ibrahim Abouleish, whom Declan had met several years earlier. Now Abouleish invited Margrit and Declan to visit Sekem and the newly founded university in Heliopolis, a suburb of Cairo.

❖ Then a few weeks later, a message arrived from Abouleish, asking whether it would suit us if he came to Steyerberg one day. We discovered – after we had agreed to it – that a neighbour knew the name Abouleish and had just bought a DVD about Sekem in an organic produce shop. We watched it and were thrilled with the project and even more thrilled to welcome its initiator a few days later. Abouleish had read my first book 'Interest and Inflation Free Money' and agreed with what I said in it. When I showed him and my grandchild Nora a short summary of a presentation, the two of them had an intense conversation about it. Seldom have I felt so completely understood and accepted. I think it is a great quality of Ibrahim Abouleish to understand and accept people".

In September 2008, the Kennedys finally travelled to Egypt. The occasion was an annual meeting of Sekem's supervisory board, which was also attended by some representatives of the German progressive GLS Bank. Margrit was asked to explain the idea of the complementary currency to them. And this was done in a three-hour workshop, during which Margrit first gave her slightly adapted standard lecture.

Music was played at intervals throughout the meeting, and there were tours through the Sekem's various districts. That which had formerly been desert, had been transformed into a blossoming, green oasis: cotton plantations, weaving, a doll production workshop, a recently expanded spice and tea processing facility, biodynamic polycultural orchards and vegetable gardens – more than half of which were laid out according to permaculture criteria. Margrit and Declan were later consulted for permaculture design, building biology and the handicap-friendly expansion of a guest house. With Margrit's help, a new ventilation system (already half-completed) was also to be implemented, in tandem with Sekem's own civil engineers.

Declan was also asked to contribute his experience from the time as Vice-President of TU Berlin to the establishment of the university in Heliopolis, while

Margrit was also engaged on the topic of "governance and equal rights for women".

***

The situation became more and more acute for the global financial and economic system. After the collapse of many banks and the resulting wave of bankruptcies this triggered, nation states also now face serious imbalances. Experts and politicians all over the world pondered how to appropriately handle the situation in order to limit the damage that has occurred and to create conditions for the recovery of the affected banks and economies.

Margrit pursued this with increasing resignation, as she often had the feeling that she was fighting against the crushing supremacy of the financial industry, which was only interested in maintaining its power. In her opinion, the opportunity this crisis and collapse created was not seized. People clung to old habits of thinking and acting, rather than trying truly new, innovative concepts to shape the way into the future.

- We are in the middle of an international financial crisis. And 'those up there' know no solution – no matter which party, no matter which country. People are unsure whether prices will not fall even further and are waiting to see whether everything will not become even cheaper tomorrow. Nobody is sure if they will get to keep their jobs. That is why people hold on to their money. It is because they hold on to their money that many companies go bankrupt. And if the companies close down, people will be unemployed. That adds to the insecurity. And so it comes full circle, and it just keeps going downhill. Regional money could stop this downward spiral. And not only that, it could turn it into an upward spiral that increases security, bit by bit."

Margrit tirelessly promoted her ideas during this period. If one reads texts she wrote during that time or hears her speak in the recordings of lectures and interviews that can be found on the internet, one easily gets an impression of how urgent a problem it seemed to her, but also how great the opportunities it presented. She worked incessantly with the initiators of the regional currencies, university lecturers, lawyers and banking experts on the theoretical foundations of complementary monetary systems.

The Last Years of Life

Yet Margrit wasn't only interested in an exchange with experts and those already involved, but also with the general public. She'd always made an effort to explain to people, in simple language and through easy-to-read texts, how the monetary system works and which flaws in it need to be recognised and corrected.

Thus, in 2011, a book was created which she hoped would see widespread distribution. At that time, a large protest movement had formed in the USA under the motto "Occupy Wall Street", which was opposed to the desperate methods of turbo-capitalism. Margrit supported this movement with great sympathy and felt reminded of the protest movements from the late 1960s, which questioned and finally overcame so much of the old. She now saw a new opportunity for far-reaching changes in the monetary and financial system, which she sought to support with straightforward explanations of what she considered important.

The manuscript that was produced, eventually comprised 400 pages. This was too long for a simple book intended for wide distribution. So she asked Stephanie Ehrenschwendtner to help her shorten it. The project was highly successful and the extensive work became an 85 page booklet. In order to assess the quality of the text, Margrit asked her daughter Antja to read it and to give her unbiased feedback. And, finally, Declan came up with the idea to call the book "Occupy Money" – based on the current protest movement.

This idea not only provided a fitting title for the book, but also a motto that stands for Margrit Kennedy's life's work. What nobody knew at that moment was that "Occupy Money" would be her last, perhaps "legacy" book. At the time Margrit wrote the book "Occupy Money", she was intensely interested in the ideas of the US-American Paul Hawken. He had discovered that a great many people were already committed to a change towards ecologically and socially meaningful ways of life, while not organized or affiliated with specific groups. Nevertheless, according to Paul Hawken, a phenomenon is occurring that suggests a united effort.

Without coordination and arrangement, millions of people worldwide are acting purposefully in a collective sense. He called this phenomenon the "immune system of the earth".

Margrit was very impressed by this concept and had it in mind when she had the idea of holding a "congress of the many" on the money topic at a central location in Germany. This would make it possible to present the key ideas to a broad public at a time when many people were shaken by the events of the crisis.

However, the initial preparatory talks ended with a disagreement among those taking part: While some wanted an open format for a non-dogmatic exchange of various initiatives and ideas, others wanted a congress dedicated exclusively to Silvio Gesell's ideas of free enterprise. Thus, two events were finally held in Leipzig in early summer 2012, one after the other. Unfortunately, Margrit, who had originally intended to take part in both events, had to cancel her participation in the free-enterprise event, as members of the right-wing political spectrum were attending. Margrit's decisive reaction to withdraw from the event reflects how sensitive she was to right-wing sentiments and politics. She was absolutely opposed to any form of nationalism and dogmatic narrowness!

***

In December 2012, Margrit and Bernard Lietaer were honoured in Sweden with the *Utstickarpriset*, a lifetime achievement award donated by the renowned

Polarbröd company, a company with a centuries-old tradition in Nordic baking culture. To receive the award, Margrit was accompanied by Declan.

Later at the second meeting with the Polarbröd group, she was accompanied by Bernard Lietaer, but also by her granddaughter Nora, with whom she had toured a European capital every year since 2006.

Together they listened to the laudatory speech, which states, "With respect for humanity and nature, Margrit Kennedy and Bernard Lietaer courageously question something fundamental for our society: how our monetary system works. For decades they have consistently demanded to rethink money, so that the money system promotes responsible use of the earth and so that investments enrich communities. Margrit Kennedy and Bernard Lietaer are brave enough to go their own way. They inspire us to think of new ways to create a society that is good for people and a productive economy, and that works within the limits of the planet.".

Her "respect for humanity and nature" and the inner strength that made Margrit so "courageous" is also well expressed in a previously unpublished, last video interview that the Austrian director and writer Johanna Tschautscher did with her in June 2013. Towards the end of the recording, Margrit speaks about how this cause is deeply connected to her heart – and one sees in this moment how much it moves her.

At the tenth anniversary of the *Chiemgauer* regional currency (June 2013), Margrit gave the keynote address and introduced Kathrin Latsch, with whom she had been working since 2009.

When Margrit had been given the diagnosis of her incurable and rapidly progressing disease in July 2013, knowing that it was time for her to prepare for her farewell to earth, she assigned Kathrin Latsch the responsibility for the administration of MonNetA. In December, MonNetA gGmbH was converted into a non-profit limited liability company for which Kathrin took over the management.

So, everything was placed in good hands. For Christmas, the family made a trip to the restaurant in the Forsthaus am Heiligenberg in the immediate vicinity of Lebensgarten. A little walk with Nora through the wintry forest was still possible for Margrit, but then she had to give up the cozy get-together in the stylish ambience of the inn. Declan brought her home, where in the early morning hours of December 28, 2013, with Declan and Antja by her side, she peacefully set off, without fear on the great journey she had looked forward to taking.

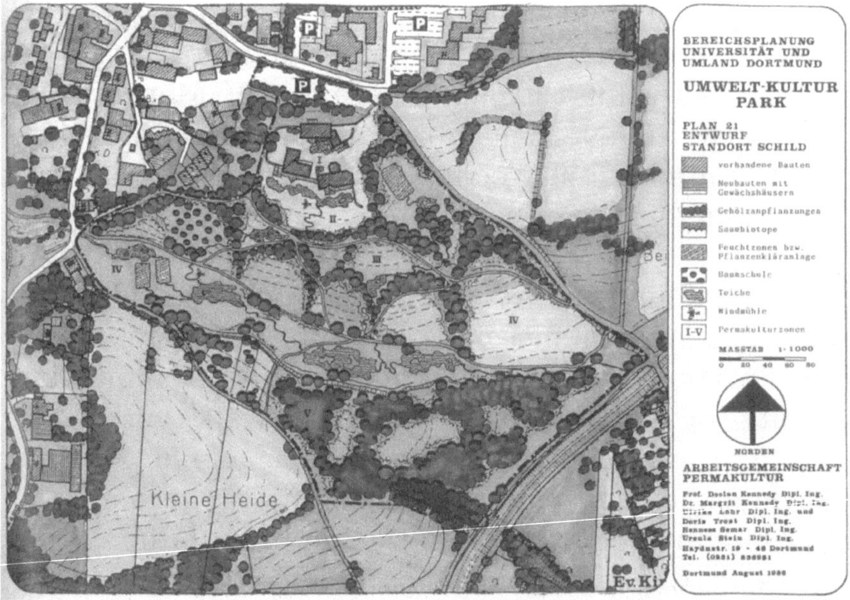

Design of the Umweltkultur (environmental) Park near the Univeristy of Dortmund, Ruhr Valley, 1986; Implementation and maintenance by a group of local residents and students, since 1987

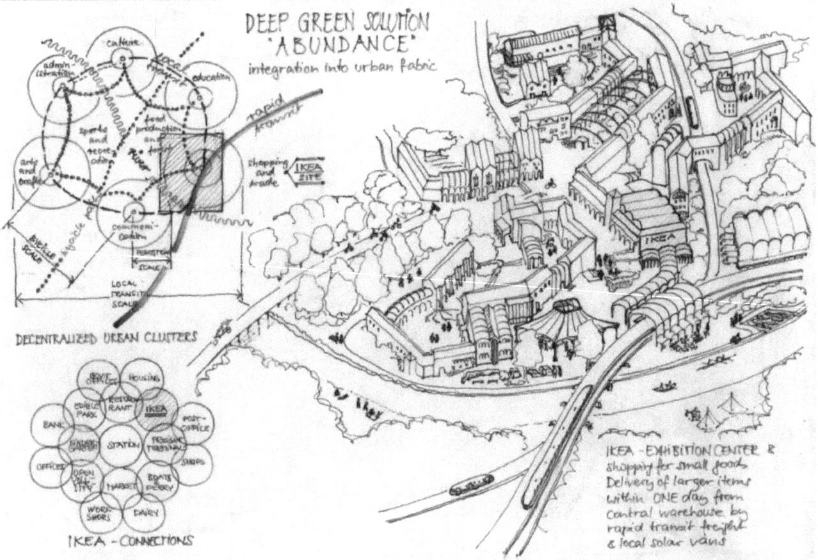

Submission to the IKEA International Design Competition with architect Frederica Miller, of Gaia Architects, Oslo, Norway

Margrit, 2000

Antja, 2005

Margrit and Declan, Ibrahim Abouileish and his civil engineer in Sekem Project near Cairo in the desert of Egypt, discussing natural ventilation for cooling buildings through earth registers, 2008

With brother Reinhard Hübner, 2010

With Nora and Declan in Athens, Greece 2010

On a TV Talk Show about Global Finance with
Tietjen & Hirschhausen, 2011

With beloved granddaughter Nora Oberländer, 2012

Last photo of Margrit Kennedy,
taken by Eva Steinebronn,
at the Christmas Eve celebration
at the Genetier/Weiler house
in Lebensgarten Steyerberg,
three days before she left this planet,
Dec. 2013

"There is a path through life, but oddly enough, you only realize it when life is over. You look back and say, 'Golly, there's a central theme.' You didn't notice it before, and yet it's there. Because you believe that all your decisions originate from free will, but that is complete nonsense! Rather, they are determined by something deep inside you, a kind of instinct; and perhaps also by karma, as your Indian friends call it. That explains everything to them, including what is inexplicable to us. (...) When you come to a fork in the road, where there is one way up and one way down, take the way up. Going downhill is less tiring, but in the end you'll end up in a hollow. To climb up is to hope. Even though it is certainly not always easy, because to see things differently is a challenge and requires constant attentiveness."

(Tiziano Terzani)

"And what really reassures me is that even though I'm gone, you'll still carry on."

(Margrit Kennedy)

Loving Life

(Epilogue by the Author)

Anyone alive today with alert senses can see that we are currently living in truly challenging times and that the prevailing trends driving these developments urgently call for new ideas and efforts that serve life. Ian Johnson, General Secretary of the Club of Rome, says: " They say that money is the root of all evil. It moves the world, but we cannot buy love with it. Indeed, money is a central feature of our existence. It is the indicator of our economic growth, our social status and our consumption habits. Two billion people on earth barely have enough money to live on, but one percent of the world's population has more money than it can ever spend, flaunting in a way that so often outrages many people." (Ian Johnson, in: "Money and Sustainability", Vienna, Berlin, Munich 2013) This illustrates in brief what lies at the root of our current dilemma. We are distracted from pursuing a mutually beneficial co-existence because we serve a monetary system that is flawed. It is therefore all the more important to ask ourselves: at what point will it become apparent that there is a dire need to renew the world's guidelines for co-existence on Mother Earth?

The fact that today's monetary system is actually the most efficient among those ever created by man makes the problem more complex. Margrit Kennedy found her challenge in precisely this. After a meeting with her architect colleague Helmut Creutz in the early 1980s, she recognized the crucial flaw in this perfectly perfidious system: the properties of interest and compound interest give money an almost magical power. It can grow in the hands of its owners without any direct effort on their part. It's no wonder that Johann Wolfgang von Goethe treated money as a diabolical invention in his drama, "Faust". Whoever thus takes on mammon, in a sense, he himself grabs the prince of the underworld by his horns.

At the end of the 1970s, writing in a small booklet, the Frenchman Gérard Klockenbring described his view of this magical power of money: "The secret power to multiply, attributed to money, is one of the most powerful imperatives in the world today, and is tacitly acknowledged by everyone. Because this power is based on an unrecognized error, it arouses the most primitive passions. The deepest awareness of life is nourished by it, even if it seems to exist through faith, ideals, inner values. As soon as this power is shaken, it causes the worst panic. It instinctively arouses ruthlessness, brutality. Since money does not "age" by its nature, as do goods, its value becomes illusory. But because this illusion is concealed through the payment of interest, all human, productive forces are subject to it. In the soul, mostly unconsciously, this is experienced as an abysmal hollowness, a sucking emptiness. This hollowness, this is mammon." (Gérard Klockenbring "Geld, Gold, Gewissen", Stuttgart 1976)

We've reached the point today where it can be said that money rules the world. But the question of who governs money actually leads to an astonishing answer: nobody! It governs itself as a system whose powers are bent on subjugating everything and anything. Since the early 1970s, Johan Galtung has referred to the violence of the system, methodically using his own heuristics to arrive at the definition of what he calls "structural violence", which he says expressly proceeds from the life of a system. The findings of medicine, mathematics and sociology enable the analysis of behaviours and processes that would otherwise be impossible to comprehend.

There's no question that a sufficiently large number of people must want and support change for any transition to succeed. It's generally hard for many to see that tomorrow's transformed world must be actively sought for and created today, by people who see that their immediate environments are directly linked to the major challenges now facing the world. The important thing is to act consciously as part of the whole. And to proactively initiate something new in one's immediate environment. In fact, this is the love of one's neighbor that Margrit Kennedy once spoke of, as she referenced the Gospel of Mark saying: "You shall love your neighbor as yourself!" (Mk. 12, 5) This sentence is a wonderful expression of matriarchal love, as Margrit understood it, because it expresses how love enables one to totally identify with another being – just like a mother's love for her child. Are we able to recognize this today? Will it become a principle to motivate general social action to a sufficient extent? What would it be like? What would we be capable of achievement from this point on, if we human beings should succeed at living in a world freed from the evil of money? If our connection to the world were a mindful and loving one? If we human beings didn't always see ourselves as competitors, but if we met each other as brothers and sisters, elders? If many of today's ideals were to become external world realities? Difficult to answer? Certainly! But it is only when we are no longer at a loss for at least a cautious answer to these questions that we will be able to escape the danger zone in which we currently find ourselves as a human community – for then we would know what to do with the freedom we hope to enjoy. We would also know the most important thing about ourselves, namely why and for what we human beings are here.

***

Six years have passed since Margrit Kennedy fell silent forever. With her work as an architect, ecologist, activist for women's rights and for a different, fair monetary system, she set things in motion. And today? In architecture and many other fields, ecological criteria now play a role that can no longer be overlooked. And a lot has also changed for the better with regard to the situation of women, although there is still a lot to do in this area.

In the global monetary system, however, a good decade after the great global crisis, everything is back to the way it was before. With recklessness and greed speculation is again widespread, as the potential lessons from the past collapse have gone unheeded. Many of the regional money initiatives that had emerged since 2003 have since disappeared from the scene. Nevertheless, Margrit Kennedy's efforts were not in vain, as increasingly more people are critically reflecting on the monetary system and looking for ways to do business in an ecologically and socially sensible way. Already it has come to the point where the small attempts and beginnings of the past will be followed by large and widely effective initiatives to create democratically administered complementary currencies. That, at any rate, is the vision that Margrit had been working towards since the 1980s. She was ahead of her time in some respects, recognising what was necessary and what was possible long before the mainstream did. When she talked about this, listeners were both impressed and enthusiastic. There was an engaging charisma in her expression that was not easy to resist.

Both Margrit and Declan Kennedy have helped to shape the global ecology movement. As a result, they've become figures of contemporary history, and through their lives and work they've set a successful and instructive example that demonstrates it is very well possible to create the conditions today that lead to the transformed world of tomorrow.

Peter Krause, Mitchell Bay (Canada), August 2019

APPENDIX

Margrit Kennedy

Lebensgarten as an example of a "Post-Growth Economy"

(A text from 2011)

The eco-village Lebensgarten Steyerberg, Germany, was established in 1985, in the 65 buildings that once comprised the living quarters of a WWII ammunition factory, built in 1939. Situated in Lower Saxony, the community is currently home to 100 adults and 40 children. The large central community building houses a cultural and social hub with offices, smaller and larger seminar rooms, a concert hall, and a canteen. In another original building, a thriving seminar center has been established, while what once a medical clinic: the "house of healing" is now a comfortable guesthouse.

In the many years we have lived in Lebensgarten, one of the greatest wonders that we have witnessed is the emergence of newfound skills among its members, developed out of necessity to compensate for the lack of specialists here, that exist in larger cities. The need to develop such skills naturally arises and leads to the discovery of a completely new quality of life. It is precisely this type of growth that is required in a *post-growth-economy*, because there is *infinite potential* in terms of "quality of life". The following examples illustrate what qualitative growth means in the context of Lebensgarten and how this conserves natural resources.

It began in 1985 with the retrofitting of the houses and the 2000 sq.m. (20,000 sq.ft.) community center. *Re-use* as opposed to *new building* resulted in a significant reduction in Lebensgarten's 'ecological footprint': e.g. building materials, energy for transport and labor hours. Each household was renovated at its own pace. There was, and there continues to be, a lot of mutual support and participation among neighbors. Each room in the community center was remodeled and financed in a different manner – some financed privately, some communally or through a combination of both options. Had we not experienced this first hand, we would not have believed it possible.

A central establishment that has been a model of success for years is Lebensgarten's food co-op, or ***Le****bensmittel* (Food) **Di**stribution Center – abbreviated "LeDi." Here, nearly all the organic food and ecologically produced supplies needed for daily living can be purchased by members at almost wholesale prices. Members each have their own key to LeDi, and can access the shop 24 hours a day, deducting the sum of their purchases from the prepaid balance maintained on their account card. This reduces the need for salespeople and for residents to drive to a market to buy groceries. It also saves on the costs of one's own food stocks.

Apart from the extensive practice among neighbors to co-operate (especially in cases of emergency), there's car-sharing – whereby a large group of residents use few cars. There is also a boutique where used items of clothing are hung, and may be taken by others free of charge. Employment opportunities, particularly in social health services and in handicrafts, are created to enable residents to work locally. Lebensgarten has also become the region's second largest "lodging business" through the seminar center's guest accommodations, in conjunction with the hosting of seminar guests by residents in their own homes. It is a nucleus for entrepreneurship and offers a setting for cooperative engagement usually found only in larger cities.

Besides dance, yoga and other exercise offerings, it is important to mention the 'pub' with its occasional discotheque. This is open Wednesday and Saturday evenings, and serves as a cafe on Sundays, where one can enjoy outstanding organic cakes baked by our own residents. Even more important than the sharing of skills, space, cars and equipment (as well as the associated cost and resource savings) is Lebensgarten's experience in conflict resolution. Violence and war present the costliest and most dire harm to life on our planet today, and hopefully will become entirely obsolete in a post-growth economy.

At Lebensgarten each person is responsible for him or herself and for the community at the same time. Nobody is required to do anything more than respect the rules of the community and pay a membership fee of 30 Euros per month to the group treasury. It's actually remarkable that Lebensgarten still actually exists – all the studies on communities suggest that it should have long ago disintegrated, due to internal conflicts. From the standpoint of social diversity, we are a microcosm of the most varied religious, spiritual, philosophical views and interests. At the same time, we are also far from homogenous in terms of our cultural origins, ages, education, incomes and professional experiences.

Most members arrive with their own ideas and ideals as to what Lebensgarten should look like and how it should function. This always creates tension because people who have not been raised in community aren't of course familiar with the ground rules for social interaction. We have had to develop these rules ourselves and they require constant renewal, as there are always new members joining the community. As a practical rule in the case of conflict, we usually try to include a neutral third party who mediates between the parties - and if that is not possible - then we try to find a resolution through a mediation process.

Thus far, we have made all the most important decisions through a "modified consensus" process. This means that if members are not in agreement with a particular decision, they are asked if they are able to live with this decision should the community proceed with it. If the answer is no, then the resolution will not be seen as passed, and the person will be asked to come up with a ratification of the decision that can then be accepted by all. If this is not possible, then the resolution cannot be passed. This method of decision making has shown itself to be more efficient and effective in the long run than the usual democratic voting process, because those who are outvoted will often find, one way or another (even if unintentional or subconscious) to circumvent or undermine the decisions that were made against their will.

Funding sources for Lebensgarten include membership fees, donations from members as well as non-members, sponsors, the earnings from the seminar center, low interest or no interest loans from neighbors and friends, and bank loans. Costs are also reduced by our own voluntary labor. Communal hands-on days are organized in such a way that it is fun to participate.
We avoid bank loans as much as possible, because our income from donations and from the proceeds of the

seminar operation is subject to fluctuations, from year to year.

Lebensgarten's kitchen offers a wonderful opportunity for residents to not have to cook themselves, and still share in tasty, healthy organic vegetarian meals, with a diverse group of people. The latest research confirms that the consumption of meat and dairy products is responsible for half of all greenhouse gas emissions. Due to energy savings in the purchase and preparation of food, there is again both cost reduction and less environmental impact for most members.

Lebensgarten also shares its knowledge with varied specialized businesses and groups in the outside world. These contacts range from vegetarian cooking classes to courses taught through the "School for Understanding and Mediation", "the Steyerberg Center for Non-Violent Communication"; from the "Forest Kindergarten", to the work of a local patient solidarity group, "Artabana", which provides an alternative to the state-mandated health insurance system.

There are women's, as well as men's groups hosted here, whose participants also come from outside the community. The many meditation forms practiced on site bring together people, from both inside and outside as well. Gaia University offers university-level, hands-on learning workshops in Lebensgarten, through permaculture and other approaches with practical application to entrepreneurial goals toward a healthy and sustainable world.

Since 2009, the production of food on our own land has increased significantly, as a result of the development of a Permaculture Park, sited directly next to Lebensgarten where vegetables, fruit and flowers are planted, grown and harvested. Ultimately, this provides a growing autonomy from the world's centralized food supply and distribution structures, enabling the conservation of resources, as well as opportunities for the restoration of nature and the maintenance of sustainable livelihoods.

We have learned that true wealth is not the accumulation of money, but is garnered through the quality of human relationships, the possibility for communication with each other on a deep level, the celebration and creation of new rituals, and the experimentation and evolution of new patterns in our relationships. The post-growth economy is not a model of 'renunciation' but one that makes us all collectively richer. Nature has been showing us how to do this successfully for millions of years. This new economy thrives on diversity not singularity; cooperation not competition. It knows no infinite growth. It's only through mutual understanding and creative connections between individuals that the potential for a healthy human society can exist. Ultimately, infinite quantitative economic growth leads only to it's own destruction. To be successful, a post-growth economy must be guided by these natural laws.

Margrit Kennedy

The Economy of Connectedness

(Preface to the German language version of "Sacred Economics", by Charles Eisenstein, 2013)

For 30 years, I have been amazed again and again by the variety of different perspectives from which the topic of "money" has been viewed, analyzed and experienced. Charles Eisenstein has added a new, extremely attractive version to the many possibilities. His proposal: the transformation of money into a means of human connection rather than separation. He reveals how money is used to create a feeling of scarcity, how it promotes greed, strengthens ruinous competition, demands endless growth and destroys communities. And he shows that in the collapse of the old world based on this system, it's possible to already find the seeds of new forms of money and cooperation that will shape our lives in the future. As an activist and researcher, philosopher, poet and spiritual seeker, he has developed this comprehensive approach, so different from anything we find in the economic mainstream, from an economic, historical and psychological perspective. One quickly sees that the simple clarity and joy he expresses in sharing the results of his research and his vision, comes from his deep understanding of the matter and is therefore rousingly credible.

In his new book, which builds on the findings of his first work *The Ascent of Humanity*, Charles Eisenstein succeeds in linking the needed changes in the human spiritual and social realm with the changes in the monetary system. He points out that money and the economy can be as "sacred", helpful, and supportive of our lives as anything else in this universe – if we design and use it accordingly. To present this in detail, and credibly, is a courageous undertaking! After all, today they appear largely the opposite of helpful and supportive – rather we feel that they are leading us into a social and economic abyss.

But Charles Eisenstein proves that despite all the chaotic upheavals we are currently experiencing, humanity is at the dawn of a new age. He shows how today's monetary system not only accelerates the upheaval, but also offers us the chance to shape it in such a way that it serves us – rather than us serving it, as before. For this, *Sacred Economics* provides solid arguments from research in the humanities and economics, but that's not all! In his book, Charles Eisenstein addresses both our hearts and minds. He gives us well-founded hope that we can recover something that we considered irretrievably lost, the oneness of all being – for he describes what he himself clearly feels, that we belong to something greater than ourselves and that this greater something, at the same time, includes ourselves.

His book helps us to understand the topic of money in its entirety, in all its depth and complexity. It allows us to better assess the various common measures, policies and options for action and their prospects of success. From this point of view, today's remedies, such as stronger financial market regulation, separation of private and investment banking, higher bank equity ratios, growth programs and debt brakes, will not be enough to deal with the crisis. Because a system in which money has to constantly grow, decoupling itself more and more from the real economy, and only enriching an increasing few (as is the case today) cannot in the long run save our democracy or the environment. For it to be used once again as a means to promote human connection rather than separation, it has to be redesigned. It must help us to bridge the gap between what we want and what we want to do, and to reintegrate spirituality into our daily lives. The German title *Economics of Solidarity* reflects this purpose very well.

In most people's minds, religion or spirituality is something set aside for Sundays and high holidays but isn't to be applied to daily life. But this, the gap between what we desire and what we do, is exactly what enables the sense of separation to grow deeper every day. Charles Eisenstein shows that there are many steps in the creation of connection that don't require one to be spiritually enlightened: carefully cultivating our friendships, peacefully resolving conflicts, participating in constructive social or cultural networks, building good neighbourly relations, supporting local currencies and autonomous economic cycles. These are just some of the ways in which everyone can help to reduce the divisive influence of money on our lives.

That we have already passed the most extreme point of separation from nature and from each other, Charles Eisenstein makes a compelling attempt to prove. And he sees the great potential of the crisis in taking us back to the beginning, when money was still a gift and served to fulfil the human longing for connectedness – and not just used as payment, thus forever creating further separation in all areas of life that once belonged together.

It is precisely this separation that today's monetary system forces upon us. Regardless of whether it is the euro, dollar or yen. All currencies are created according to the same principle. Money is created, for the most part, as credit by commercial banks. Because of the necessity to promote debt for the earning of compound interest, all monetary systems are programmed for constant, i.e. exponential or pathological growth. This represents a first systemic flaw. This results at regular intervals in "money bubbles" that inevitably burst, a second serious flaw. And as a third evil, the accumulation of interest permanently redistributes money from bottom to top, from the vast majority who work for it to a small minority who allow the money to "work" for itself.

However, money cannot perform work. Only humans or machines can do that. Yet, the world continues to suffer from this illusion.

Since all the changes that we can realistically demand are too insufficient to help us fulfill our dream of realizing our highest potential on earth, Eisenstein logically argues for the "unrealistic" – for a gift economy. He shows that we have been part of a gift economy since we were born, because we are given the most valuable thing in our life: life itself, the earth, nature, the air, people we love, the beauty of flowers and stars the song of the birds, the cultural heritage of humanity, our stories, fairy tales and songs and much more.

In expert detail, Charles Eisenstein outlines how our monetary system is taking more and more of these gifts, privatizing and commercializing them, making a few ever richer, while evermore impoverishing the vast majority. Standing before the remains of untouched nature, buildings or works of art that were created centuries or millennia ago, we sometimes suddenly realize how cheap and ugly everything has become, as the monetary system is subject to the principle of "make more money out of money". Therefore, a central question of the book is: can we introduce a monetary system that's better than the current one? One that serves the vast majority of people, and not just the small minority of wealthy people who benefit from today's system?

Charles Eisenstein vigorously affirms that we can, sharing his confidence in the numerous new models in every country of the world exploring how to deal differently with money. His extensive evidence, always peppered with exciting details, shows that this monetary system is not God-given, but was developed by people and, therefore, can be changed by people so that it's possible to fulfill our dream of a more beautiful world.

When I first met Charles Eisenstein, personally, at a conference in Munich in the summer of 2012, I had only read a few articles by him and seen a few films. But I was immediately won over by the clarity, courage, wisdom and persuasive attitude with which he expressed his desire to create the world our hearts dream of. Seldom have I met a person who can so precisely illuminate all the ups and downs – even better still, the shallows – of the topic of money with such a broad spectrum of human experience and development.

Although he's not afraid to use technical language, his articles, books and lectures remain generally understandable. Even in his sharp criticism, he is never hurtful towards the people or issues concerned. His great strength is that he always returns to his analysis of the fundamental mistake in our worldview: the illusion of separation from each other and from nature. He lets us take part in his journey of discovery, through the development of our civilization, to show the important role money has always played: both for the achievement of cultural excellence, which we rightly admire, and for the destruction of our natural environment, through which we all suffer.

In this book, Charles Eisenstein takes up the work of important thought leaders who have interpreted and described money as a social construct. And he arrives (as I did 30 years ago, as well as many other authors) at a solution to the mistakes in today's system; the suggestion by Silvio Gesell that there out to be a circulation impulse on money (in the jargon "demurrage") or "negative interest". In his view, only a monetary system that is not based on today's interest-based growth constraint can be fair, durable and stable, since a negative interest rate allows productive investment even at interest rates around zero or below zero. Moreover, such a monetary system overcomes the fundamental error of neoliberal economics to see money as a neutral veil over economic activity. It is equally important to overcome the assumption that the so-called *homo oeconomicus* is controlled by economic rationality. Giving and receiving gifts corresponds much more closely to human nature, and only the recognition and legitimisation of this need will, in Eisenstein's view, produce a society that is worthy of human beings and worth living in. I agree with this, because it corresponds to my thirty years of experience of living in a community of 100 adults and 40 children.

In the numerous new models for complementary currencies, Charles Eisenstein sees further possibilities for transforming money into what it was originally invented to be. With expertise and empathy, he describes the struggle for recognition that these initiatives still have to fight in an environment of power structures that do everything to preserve the old.

Overall, the book is invaluable in its wealth of detail and technical accuracy through observations, analysis and evidence. It aims to get straight to the heart of today's plight: the unequal distribution of resources in the world. In contrast to many other authors, Charles Eisenstein also makes it clear to the privileged classes how much better off they would be if they were involved in the urgently necessary amendments, but also in the implementation of our collective dream of a more just and more beautiful world, because our visions today are the realities of tomorrow.

Presented logically, and through practical and illustrative examples, the hope and confidence-generating power of the book is rooted in the fact that we are all better off in a gift economy. With this approach, Charles Eisenstein first became one of the pioneers of the Occupy movement in the United States and he is well on the way to becoming such a pioneer in Europe. His book is a gift to all who feel connected to nature and culture, who think ahead and who are ready to implement better practical solutions together.

Margrit Kennedy, 2013

Translated from Charles Eisenstein:
ÖKONOMIE DER VERBUNDENHEIT (Economy of Solidarity – How money led the world to the abyss – and yet can save it now). Scorpio Verlag GmbH & Co. KG, Berlin / Munich, 2013

More articles and books in many languages by Margrit Kennedy to be found and some to be downloaded on the following websites:

margritkennedy.de/en/
kennedy-library.info
monneta.org/en/

About the Author

Peter Krause is a freelance journalist and writer. His main areas of focus are medicine, economics and the writing of biographies. In addition to his professional interest in ecologically oriented business and forms of money, he is particularly interested in the meaningful experience of nature. He believes that a sound economy and a holistic ecology are inseparably linked.

aktiv-zukunft-leben.de

About the Translator

Elisa Graf, born in San Francisco, is a 4th generation Californian who has lived in Germany with her husband and two children since 2010. A writer and translator, she's also a regular contributor to Share International magazine reporting on issues of social justice and world change. Motivated by her deep interest in sustainability, community-building and meditation, she delights in helping others express their progressive vision for the world.

elisagraf.com

ISBN 978-3-7531-0680-9
9 783753 106809 00001
www.epubli.de